Introduction to Daily Language Review

Why Daily Language Review?

The premise behind *Daily Language Review* is simple and straightforward—frequent, focused practice leads to mastery and retention of the skills practiced.

What's in Daily Language Review?

The book is divided into 36 weekly sections. There are five practice items for each day of the week.

Monday through Thursday follow this format:

- two sentences to edit—corrections need to be made in punctuation, capitalization, and grammar.

- three items that practice a variety of language and reading skills.

Friday's practice cycles through five formats:

- identifying mistakes—deciding if marked sections of a reading passage contain punctuation, capitalization, and spelling errors.

- combining sentences—two simple sentences are combined to form one more sophisticated sentence

- language usage practice—choosing the correct verb form, pronoun, homophone, etc. to use in a sentence.

- reference materials—choosing whether to use an encyclopedia, almanac, dictionary, thesaurus, or phone book to find information.

- figurative speech—giving definitions for figures of speech.

An Answer Key for each week is provided on the same page as the Friday lesson.

Scope and sequence charts on pages 3 and 4 detail the specific skills practiced and show in which weeks the practice occurs. The skills included are those found in language texts at this level.

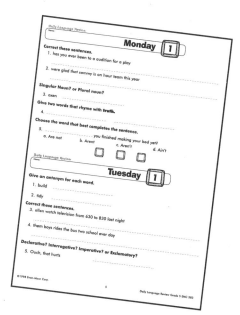

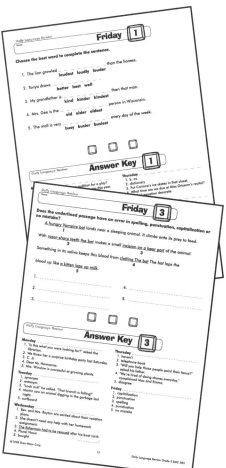

Daily Language Review Grade 5 EMC 583

How to Use *Daily Language Review*

There are several ways that the daily review practices can be presented. You may want to use all of these presentations throughout the year to help keep the practice fresh and interesting.

1. Make overhead transparencies of the lessons. Conduct the practice as an oral activity with the entire class. Write answers and make corrections using an erasable pen.

   Increased retention of the skill will occur if students mark the answers at the same time on a reproduced sheet or write the answer on writing paper. As the class becomes more familiar with *Daily Language Review*, you may want students to mark their own answers first and then check responses by marking the items on the transparency.

2. Reproduce the pages for individuals or partners to work independently. Check answers as a group using an overhead transparency to model the correct answers.

   Use these pages as independent practice only after much oral group experience with the lessons.

3. Occasionally you may want to use a day's, or even a week's, lesson as a test to see how individuals are progressing in their acquisition of skills.

It should be stressed, however, that the greatest learning benefit will be gained from doing the practices orally so that students continually hear correct responses modeled by their classmates and the teacher.

Hints, Suggestions, and Options

1. Look ahead several weeks at the skills being practiced. If possible, teach new skills in formal lessons before asking students to practice these skills in the daily review.

2. Sometimes you will not have taught a given skill before it appears in a lesson. These items should then be done together. Tell the class that there is a skill they have not yet been taught. See if anyone knows the answer and wishes to explain it to the class. If not, use the review time to conduct a mini-lesson on that skill.

3. Customize the daily review lessons to the needs of your class.

   • If there are skills that are not included in the grade level expectancies of the particular program you teach, you may choose to skip those items—white them out or correct them before reproducing the page.

   • If you feel your class needs more practice than is provided, add these "extras" on your own. For example:

      Use the daily "edit" sentences to locate subject, predicate, parts of speech, etc.

      Add a one-item warm up, a mini-post test, or ask students to provide another example.

Skills Scope and Sequence

Punctuation & Grammar

Week	Abbreviations	Misc. Punctuation	Comparative/Superlative Adj.	Common/Proper Nouns	Language Usage	Parts of Speech	Possessive Nouns	Prepositional Phrase	Sentence Types	Singular/Plural Nouns	Subject/Object Pronouns	Subject/Predicate	Type of Adjective	Type of Adverb	Verb Tense
Week 1	x				x				x	x					
Week 2						x									
Week 3	x									x					x
Week 4					x	x									x
Week 5	x				x	x	x		x					x	x
Week 6					x							x	x		x
Week 7						x									
Week 8		x				x									
Week 9	x										x				
Week 10				x					x	x		x			x
Week 11			x	x	x										
Week 12			x	x	x	x									
Week 13					x	x						x			
Week 14					x	x				x	x	x			x
Week 15	x					x				x				x	x
Week 16		x			x	x			x	x	x				
Week 17		x		x	x			x				x			
Week 18				x	x				x		x		x		
Week 19					x		x		x					x	x
Week 20	x	x				x				x					
Week 21					x						x				x
Week 22	x					x	x	x				x			
Week 23					x		x						x	x	x
Week 24		x			x	x				x	x	x		x	
Week 25		x	x			x	x								
Week 26	x		x	x	x	x		x				x			
Week 27						x				x	x				x
Week 28						x						x	x		
Week 29	x		x		x			x	x		x				
Week 30	x		x			x							x		x
Week 31												x		x	
Week 32						x	x								
Week 33						x		x				x	x		
Week 34	x			x	x					x				x	
Week 35			x									x	x		x
Week 36	x			x					x						

Comprehension

Week	Analogies	Categorizing	Cause and Effect	Fact/Fantasy/Fiction/Nonfiction	Fact/Opinion	Figure of Speech	Inference	Similes/Metaphors	Word Meaning from Context
Week 1	x						x		
Week 2				x				x	x
Week 3		x	x			x			
Week 4					x		x		
Week 5			x			x			
Week 6	x			x					x
Week 7		x						x	
Week 8	x	x			x				x
Week 9	x	x					x		
Week 10				x	x	x	x		
Week 11		x	x					x	
Week 12	x				x				x
Week 13	x				x				
Week 14						x			x
Week 15	x	x				x		x	
Week 16			x	x					
Week 17	x				x				
Week 18				x					x
Week 19	x	x					x		
Week 20			x			x		x	x
Week 21	x		x	x			x		
Week 22									x
Week 23		x			x				x
Week 24						x		x	
Week 25	x		x		x	x			
Week 26			x			x			x
Week 27		x					x		
Week 28				x	x			x	x
Week 29	x		x		x				
Week 30									x
Week 31		x	x		x	x	x		x
Week 32		x					x	x	
Week 33	x	x				x			x
Week 34					x		x		x
Week 35	x	x		x					
Week 36					x		x	x	

Vocabulary/Word Study Skills

Week	Base Words/Prefixes/Suffixes	Contractions	Homophones	Phonics	Rhyme	Synonyms/Antonyms
Week 1	x	x			x	x
Week 2				x		x
Week 3	x	x				x
Week 4		x	x		x	x
Week 5						x
Week 6	x	x	x		x	
Week 7	x		x			x
Week 8		x				
Week 9				x	x	x
Week 10		x	x			
Week 11	x			x	x	x
Week 12						x
Week 13		x		x		x
Week 14	x					
Week 15	x					x
Week 16	x		x			
Week 17		x	x			x
Week 18			x			
Week 19	x					
Week 20			x			
Week 21	x			x	x	x
Week 22	x					x
Week 23						x
Week 24		x	x			x
Week 25	x		x			
Week 26						
Week 27	x			x	x	x
Week 28	x					
Week 29				x	x	
Week 30			x			x
Week 31					x	x
Week 32	x	x	x			x
Week 33	x					
Week 34						
Week 35	x	x				x
Week 36	x					x

Reference Skills

Week	Alphabetical Order	Dictionary Guide Words	Reference Materials	Syllabication
Week 1			x	x
Week 2	x		x	x
Week 3			x	
Week 4	x			
Week 5				x
Week 6			x	
Week 7			x	x
Week 8	x			
Week 9			x	x
Week 10	x	x		
Week 11				x
Week 12			x	
Week 13			x	x
Week 14				
Week 15		x		
Week 16		x	x	x
Week 17			x	
Week 18		x		
Week 19				x
Week 20	x		x	
Week 21		x		
Week 22	x		x	x
Week 23		x		
Week 24				
Week 25			x	x
Week 26				
Week 27	x		x	
Week 28				x
Week 29			x	x
Week 30			x	
Week 31				
Week 32	x	x		
Week 33			x	
Week 34		x		x
Week 35			x	x
Week 36		x		x

Other Language Skills

Week	Correct/Incorrect Spelling	Friendly/Business Letter	Identify the Mistake	Sentence Combination
Week 1				
Week 2				
Week 3		x	x	
Week 4	x			x
Week 5				
Week 6	x			
Week 7	x			
Week 8	x	x	x	
Week 9	x			x
Week 10				
Week 11		x		
Week 12	x			
Week 13	x		x	
Week 14		x		x
Week 15	x			
Week 16				
Week 17	x			
Week 18		x	x	
Week 19	x			x
Week 20	x		x	
Week 21				
Week 22	x			
Week 23		x	x	
Week 24				x
Week 25				
Week 26		x		
Week 27				
Week 28	x		x	
Week 29		x		
Week 30	x			
Week 31	x		x	
Week 32	x			x
Week 33				
Week 34	x			
Week 35	x			
Week 36	x		x	

Sentence Editing Skills

Capitalization
- Beginning of Sentence
- Books, Songs, Poems, Titles of People
- Other Proper Nouns

Punctuation
- End of Sentence
- Period Abbreviations, Initials
- Colon in Time
- Underline Books, Magazines
- Run-on Sentences

Quotation Marks
- In Speech
- Songs, Poems, Short Stories

Comma
- Words in a Series
- Dates, Addresses
- To Separate Dialogue
- Direct Address/Interjection
- Compound Sentence
- After Introductory Phrase/Clause
- Nonrestrictive Appositive
- Between Coordinate Adjectives

Apostrophe
- Contractions
- Possessives

Grammar & Usage
- Correct Article/Adjective/Adverb
- Homophones
- Double Negatives
- Plurals
- Pronouns
- Verb Forms

Weeks tracked: Week 1 through Week 36

Monday 1

Correct these sentences.

1. has you ever been to a audition for a play

2. were glad that sammy is on hour team this year

Singular or plural?

3. oxen

Give two words that rhyme with truth.

4.

Choose the word that best completes the sentence.

5. _____ you finished making your bed yet?

Are not   Arent   Aren't   Ain't

Tuesday 1

Give an antonym for each word.

1. build

2. tidy

Correct these sentences.

3. allen watch television from 630 to 830 last night

4. them boys rides the bus two school ever day

Declarative, interrogative, imperative, or exclamatory?

5. Ouch, that hurts

Wednesday 1

Correct these sentences.

1. werent their no cookies left

2. why cant jerome never get here on time

Complete the analogy.

3. height : inches :: weight : _____

Where will the following probably take place?

4. The umpire yelled, "You're out!"

What is the root or base word?

5. illegal

Thursday 1

What is the correct abbreviation for ounce?

1. a. ou.   b. oz.   c. oun.   d. none of these

What reference source would you use to find the meaning of etiquette?

2. _____

Correct these sentences.

3. put corinnes ice skates in that there closet

4. what time are we do at miss grissoms recital

Which words have three syllables?

5. vertical   equation   temperature   decorate

Name: _____

Friday **1**

Choose the best word to complete the sentence.

1. The lion growled _____ than the lioness.

               loudest   loudly   louder

2. Tonya draws _____ .

            better   best   well

3. My grandfather is _____ than that man.

           kind   kinder   kindest

4. Mrs. Gee is the _____ person in Wisconsin.

          old   older   oldest

5. The mall is very _____ every day of the week.

        busy   busier   busiest

Daily Language Review

Answer Key **1**

Monday
1. Have you ever been to an audition for a play?
2. We're glad that Sammy is on our team this year.
3. plural noun
4. Answers will vary.
5. Aren't

Tuesday
1. destroy
2. messy
3. Allen watched television from 6:30 to 8:30 last night.
4. Those boys ride the bus to school every day.
5. exclamatory

Wednesday
1. Weren't there any cookies left?
2. Why can't Jerome get here on time?
3. pounds or ounces
4. at the ball park
5. legal

Thursday
1. b. oz.
2. dictionary
3. Put Corinne's ice skates in that closet.
4. What time are we due at Miss Grissom's recital?
5. vertical, equation, decorate

Friday
1. louder
2. well
3. kinder
4. oldest
5. busy

Monday 2

Correct these sentences.

1. we dont got no pets in our family

_____

2. kelsey said i want to go to aunt joys for thanksgiving

_____

Use context clues to determine the meaning of the bolded word below.

3. **Catastrophes**, including floods and earthquakes, did great damage to the farm town.

_____

Fact or fiction?

4. A moose strips off and eats the bark of trees.

5. The herd of moose danced in a circle in the middle of the stream.

Tuesday 2

Give a synonym for respond.

1. _____

Which word would come first in alphabetical order?

2. amuse   address   Arab   antler   actor

Correct these sentences.

3. i havent never been to a professional football game

_____

4. i wont eat spinach and beets for dinner shouted maurice

_____

Write the pronoun that would replace the underlined nouns.

5. <u>Ernie</u> and <u>Fred</u> went scuba diving in Florida.

Wednesday 2

Correct these sentences.

1. please put a ice cube in there lemonade

....

2. mr mastin asked whose ordering school lunch today

....

What do you call this part of a friendly letter?

3. Love, ...

Simile or metaphor?

4. The old man's hair was <u>as white as snow</u>.

Circle the adverb in this sentence.

5. Treat the new kitten gently so you don't injure it.

Thursday 2

Which word would come last in alphabetical order?

1. together   the   twice   tiger   turkey

How many syllables does this word have?

2. decoration ....

Correct these sentences.

3. does the music start at 400 or 430 inquired Ms Clark

....

4. the workmen has come to repair the roof on hermans house

....

Which words have the same sound as /sh/ in wish?

5. sure   occasion   mission   official

Name:

Friday 2

Which reference source would be best to look up the information: thesaurus, dictionary, telephone book, atlas, encyclopedia, or almanac?

1. in which country is the Amazon River

2. an antonym for the word "awkward"

3. the address of your doctor's office

4. how to pronounce the word "mischievous"

5. information on the District of Columbia

Daily Language Review

Answer Key 2

Monday
1. We don't have any pets in our family.
2. Kelsey said, "I want to go to Aunt Joy's for Thanksgiving."
3. Catastrophes are terrible disasters.
4. fact
5. fiction

Tuesday
1. answer, reply
2. actor
3. I haven't ever been to a professional football game.
4. "I won't eat spinach and beets for dinner!" shouted Maurice.
5. they

Wednesday
1. Please put an ice cube in their lemonade.
2. Mr. Mastin asked, "Who's ordering school lunch today?"
3. closing
4. simile
5. gently

Thursday
1. twice
2. four
3. "Does the music start at 4:00 or 4:30?" inquired Ms. Clark.
4. The workmen have come to repair the roof on Herman's house.
5. sure   mission   official

Friday
1. atlas, encyclopedia
2. thesaurus
3. telephone book
4. dictionary
5. almanac, encyclopedia

Monday 3

Correct these sentences.

1. is this what you was looking for asked the librarian

2. we throwed her an surprise birthday party last saturday

What is the correct abbreviation for Junior?

3. a. Jun.　　　　b. Jr　　　　c. Jr.　　　　d. none of these

Find the salutation for a business letter.

4. Dear Bill,　　　　Dear Mr. Hermanns:　　　　Dear Mrs. Lee,

What is the meaning of this figure of speech?

5. Everyone who sees Mrs. Winslow's garden says she <u>has a green thumb</u>.

Tuesday 3

Synonyms or antonyms?

1. terrible, awful

2. clumsy, graceful

Correct these sentences.

3. look out he called that branch is falling

4. martin saw a animal digging in the garbage last knight

Which word does not belong in this group?

5. bird　　　plane　　　surfboard　　　kite　　　hot-air balloon

　　　11

Wednesday 3

Correct these sentences.

1. rev and mrs boyton is excited about there vacation plans

2. she dont need no help with her homework assignment

Circle the cause and underline the effect.

3. The fisherman had to be rescued after his boat sank.

Singular or plural?

4. people

Give the past tense of the verb buy.

5.

Thursday 3

What contraction is made from these two words?

1. have not

What reference source would you use to find the address of the nearest music store?

2.

Correct these sentences.

3. will you help them people paint theyre fence asked his father

4. were tired of doing chores every day complained max and emma

Add a prefix to the word.

5. agree

Name:

Friday 3

Read the following paragraph and decide if the underlined parts have a capitalization error, a punctuation error, a spelling error, or no mistake.

A hungry Vampire bat lands near a sleeping animal. It climbs onto its prey to feed.
        1

With razor-sharp teeth the bat makes a small incision on a bear part of the animal.
      2   **3**

Something in its saliva keeps this blood from clotting The bat laps the blood up
                                                    4

like a kitten laps up milk.
     5

1. _____   4. _____

2. _____   5. _____

3. _____

Answer Key 3

Monday
1. "Is this what you were looking for?" asked the librarian.
2. We threw her a surprise birthday party last Saturday.
3. c. Jr.
4. Dear Mr. Hermanns:
5. Mrs. Winslow is successful at growing plants.

Tuesday
1. synonyms
2. antonyms
3. "Look out!" he called. "That branch is falling!"
4. Martin saw an animal digging in the garbage last night.
5. surfboard

Wednesday
1. Rev. and Mrs. Boyton are excited about their vacation plans.
2. She doesn't need any help with her homework assignment.
3. The fisherman had to be rescued after his boat sank.
4. plural
5. bought

Thursday
1. haven't
2. telephone book
3. "Will you help those people paint their fence?" asked his father.
4. "We're tired of doing chores every day," complained Max and Emma.
5. disagree

Friday
1. capitalization
2. no mistake
3. spelling
4. punctuation
5. no mistake

Monday 4

Correct these sentences.

1. on may 26 1998 my brother will graduate from illinois college

_____

2. is you gonna be finish with your report by friday

_____

Give the past tense for the verb worry.

3. _____

Write a fact about this topic: broccoli

4. _____

Give an antonym for seldom.

5. _____

Tuesday 4

Choose the best word to complete the sentence.

1. He _____ have any brothers or sisters.

    don't   doesn't   wasn't   never

Correct these sentences.

2. i red a amazing story about the hardships of sum early travelers

_____

3. we needs to be at the airport by 945 or well miss hour flight

_____

What two words make up the contraction?

4. won't _____

Use this homophone pair in one sentence. (they're, there)

5. _____

Wednesday [4]

Correct these sentences.

1. after she lies the eggs the hen sets on them

_____

2. shawna can run fastest then anyone else i no

_____

Circle the adjectives in this sentence.

3. The extraterrestrial had enormous green eyes and long, pointed antennae on its slimy head.

Give two words that rhyme with heard.

4. _____

Which word IS spelled correctly?

5. ourselfs   areselfs   ourselves   areselves

☐   ☐   ☐

Thursday [4]

Which word would come first in alphabetical order?

1. duckling   ostrich   flamingo   dove   dormouse

Where is someone who is saying the following?

2. "Flight 328 for London now leaving at Gate 37."

Correct these sentences.

3. are eight puppys is growing bigger every day explained tito

_____

4. is miss bishops sunday school class gonna sing o little town of bethlehem in the pageant

_____

What part of speech is underlined – noun, verb, adjective, or adverb?

5. Come home <u>quickly</u> after school so Grandma can see you before she leaves.

Name: _____

Friday 4

Combine the sentences to make one sentence.

1. The picnic lasted until 5:00.   It began to rain at 5:00.

   _____

2. Most of the farmers grow corn on their farms.
   The crops grow during the summer months.

   _____

3. Whales swim great distances.   They dive for food along the way.

   _____

4. The hurricane destroyed many homes.   It did not damage the city hall.

   _____

5. The President was at the conference dinner.   He gave a long speech after dinner.

   _____

Answer Key 4

Monday
1. On May 26, 1998, my brother will graduate from Illinois College.
2. Are you going to be finished with your report by Friday?
3. worried
4. Answers will vary.
5. often

Tuesday
1. doesn't
2. I read an amazing story about the hardships of some early travelers.
3. We need to be at the airport by 9:45 or we'll miss our flight.
4. will not
5. Answers will vary.

Wednesday
1. After she lays her eggs, the hen sits on them.
2. Shawna can run faster than anyone else I know.
3. enormous, green, long, pointed, slimy
4. Answers will vary.
5. ourselves

Thursday
1. dormouse
2. at an airport
3. "Our eight puppies are growing bigger every day," explained Tito.
4. Is Miss Bishop's Sunday School class going to sing "O, Little Town of Bethlehem" in the pageant?
5. adverb

Friday
Sentences may vary somewhat. Accept any reasonable sentence construction that contains all the information.
1. The picnic lasted until 5:00 when it began to rain.
   OR
   The picnic lasted until it began to rain at 5:00.
2. Most of the farmers grow corn on their farms during the summer months.
3. Whales swim great distances, diving for food along the way.
4. The hurricane destroyed many homes, but did not damage the city hall.
5. The President gave a long speech after the conference dinner.

Monday   5

Correct these sentences.

1. dont put youre feet on the furniture said grandmother

2. this doesnt look like nothing ive ever seen before

Give the possessive noun.

3. the new coat belonging to Sharon

Choose the best word to complete the sentence.

4. Mr. Tan gave _____ each five dollars for helping clean out his garage.

those   these   them   their

What is the meaning of this figure of speech?

5. You'd better <u>button up your lip</u>.

Tuesday   5

What is the correct way to divide this word into syllables?

1. coll ar   col lar   co llar

Does the underlined adverb tell how, when, where, or to what extent?

2. The tortoise moved <u>slowly</u> down the path.

Correct these sentences.

3. dont touch that read hot skillet

4. lupe asked why doesnt he never do his homework

Circle the cause and underline the effect.

5. Ito had to get a tetanus shot after he stepped on a rusty nail.

Wednesday 5

Correct these sentences.

1. mavis ate most of her salad but she left a orange slice

_____

2. dr conrads wife margaret will join him at the ceremony

_____

Which part of speech is underlined – noun, verb, adjective, or adverb?

3. She picked a <u>delicious</u> peach from the tree. _____

Synonyms or antonyms?

4. generous, stingy _____

What is the correct abbreviation for Ohio?

5. Oh.   O   OH   Ohi.

□   □   □

Thursday 5

What are the past and future tense of the verb plan?

1. past _____   future _____

Give the possessive noun.

2. eggs belonging to that bird _____

Correct these sentences.

3. was the musicians nervous before the concert begun

_____

4. mildred picked an peach from the tree it were delicious

_____

Declarative, interrogative, imperative, or exclamatory?

5. After the ceremony was over, everyone went out to celebrate. _____

What do the underlined phrases mean?

1. Is dinner ready yet? I could <u>eat a horse</u>.

2. Dad was <u>racking his brain</u> trying to remember where he left the car keys.

3. My sister <u>swims like a fish</u>.

4. Oh, dear, we're <u>up the creek without a paddle</u>.

5. I can't believe you did that. Are you <u>off your rocker</u>?

Monday
1. "Don't put your feet on the furniture," said Grandmother.
2. This doesn't look like anything I've ever seen before.
3. Sharon's new coat
4. them
5. It means to keep quiet or to not say anything.

Tuesday
1. col lar
2. how
3. Don't touch that red hot skillet!
4. Lupe asked, "Why doesn't he ever do his homework?"
5. <u>Ito had to get a tetanus shot</u> after (he stepped on a rusty nail.)

Wednesday
1. Mavis ate most of her salad, but she left an orange slice.
2. Dr. Conrad's wife, Margaret, will join him at the ceremony.
3. adjective
4. antonyms
5. OH

Thursday
1. planned   will plan
2. that bird's eggs
3. Were the musicians nervous before the concert began?
4. Mildred picked a peach from the tree. It was delicious.
5. declarative

Friday
1. I'm very hungry
2. really concentrating
3. is a very good swimmer
4. having great difficulty; have a serious problem
5. doing something that isn't sensible; acting irrationally

Monday 6

Correct these sentences.

1. do you want mustard onions pickles or sauerkraut on your hot dog

2. this peace of pizza is two hot too eat

Use context clues to determine the meaning of the bolded word below.

3. Brendon's mother took him to the **dermatologist** when he developed a strange rash on his face.

Give two words that rhyme with the word rough.

4.

Fiction or nonfiction?

5. Every year on St. Patrick's Day, leprechauns dance in the moonlight at midnight.

Tuesday 6

Does the underlined adjective tell which one, what kind, or how many?

1. <u>That</u> large, spotted cow ran away from the farmer.

Give the predicate of the following sentence.

2. A large, gray cat jumped on top of the brick wall.

Correct these sentences.

3. there grandfather baked cookies and the children eight them all

4. how good did you due on the test tanisha ask

Which word is NOT spelled correctly?

5. ocean   owner   obay   orchestra

Wednesday 6

Correct these sentences.

1. will you put all them books on the top shelf

_____

2. ben jerry and albert saw a movie called invaders from outer space saturday afternoon

_____

Complete the analogy.

3. 100 : meter :: 36 : _____

What reference source would you use to find a synonym for angry?

4. _____

Synonyms, antonyms, or homophones?

5. byte, bite _____

Thursday 6

What contraction is made from these two words?

1. they are _____

Add a prefix to this word.

2. able _____

Correct these sentences.

3. kelly didnt have no lunch today

_____

4. my friend katrina moved to seattle washington recently

_____

Past, present, or future?

5. applied _____

Friday 6

Choose the best word to complete each sentence.

1. It's not wise to _____ expensive personal items to school.
   taked   bring   took   brought

2. A limousine _____ behind our car.
   park   is park   parked   parking

3. It will take at least four hours to _____ this assignment.
   finished   done   complete   doing

4. _____ be late for her appointment.
   She's   She   She'll   Her'll

5. The space station _____ been hit by a meteor.
   gots   have   has   gonna

Daily Language Review

Answer Key 6

Monday
1. Do you want mustard, onions, pickles, or sauerkraut on your hot dog?
2. This piece of pizza is too hot to eat.
3. a doctor specializing in skin diseases
4. Answers will vary.
5. fiction

Tuesday
1. which one
2. jumped on top of the brick wall
3. Their grandfather baked cookies, and the children ate them all.
4. "How well did you do on the test?" Tanisha asked.
5. obay (obey)

Wednesday
1. Will you put all those books on the top shelf?
2. Ben, Jerry, and Albert saw a movie called <u>Invaders from Outer Space</u> Saturday afternoon.
3. yard
4. thesaurus or dictionary
5. homophone

Thursday
1. they're
2. unable, disable
3. Kelly didn't have any lunch today.
4. My friend Katrina moved to Seattle, Washington, recently.
5. past

Friday
1. bring
2. parked
3. complete
4. She'll
5. has

Monday 7

Correct these sentences.

1. did you ride on won of the paddle boats along the missouri river

_____

2. larry shouted look at that

_____

Use this homophone pair in one sentence. (band, banned)

3. _____

Circle the preposition in this sentence.

4. He found the puppy under the porch.

Give another word that would belong in this group.

5. mauve   puce   indigo   aqua

          ☐   ☐   ☐

Tuesday 7

Give an antonym for this word.

1. unique _____

Which word is NOT spelled correctly?

2. they're   thier   there   their

Correct these sentences.

3. snails aphids and mites nibbled on the plants in aunt maybelles garden

_____

4. we like hot whether we always goes to the beach to swim

_____

Does this word have a prefix or a suffix?

5. agreement _____

Wednesday 7

Correct these sentences.

1. cherie thought i hope he choose me to bee in the play

_____

2. sometimes i feels like playing with my friends and sometimes i doesnt

_____

What is the root or base word?

3. misbehaving _____

Simile or metaphor?

4. Max can always fool us because he is <u>as sly as a fox</u>. _____

Circle the adverb in this sentence.

5. Mr. Morris worked patiently with the new student.

Thursday 7

How many syllables are in each word?

1. intersection _____

2. occurring _____

Correct these sentences.

3. you musnt play until after you done your chores

_____

4. i may try out four soccer or i may join the track team

_____

Write the pronoun that would replace the underlined words in this sentence.

5. That football belongs to <u>Mark and me</u>. _____

Friday 7

Which reference source would be best to look up the information: thesaurus, dictionary, telephone book, atlas, encyclopedia, or almanac?

1. how to pronounce "arboreal"

2. another word for "famished"

3. what language "amnesia" comes from

4. a picture of a galleon

5. the city located at 30 N latitude, 90 W longitude

Answer Key 7

Monday
1. Did you ride on one of the paddle boats along the Missouri River?
2. Larry shouted, "Look at that!"
3. Answers will vary.
4. under
5. Answers will vary.

Tuesday
1. ordinary, usual
2. thier (their)
3. Snails, aphids, and mites nibbled on the plants in Aunt Maybelle's garden.
4. We like hot weather. We always go to the beach to swim.
5. suffix

Wednesday
1. Cherie thought, "I hope he chooses me to be in the play."
2. Sometimes I feel like playing with my friends and sometimes I don't.
3. behave
4. simile
5. patiently

Thursday
1. 4
2. 3
3. You mustn't play until after you have done (or do) your chores.
4. I may try out for soccer, or I may join the track team.
5. us

Friday
1. dictionary
2. thesaurus, dictionary
3. dictionary
4. dictionary, encyclopedia
5. atlas

Monday 8

Correct these sentences.

1. his parents went to a chinese restaurant to celebrate there anniversary

_____

2. prof w c wilson and his wife were both born on january 16 1965

_____

Is the comma used correctly?

3. June 16, 1940 _____

4. Memphis Tennessee, 43609 _____

Which part of speech is underlined – noun, verb, adjective, or adverb?

5. Ali and Giorgio met to pick <u>berries</u> in a nearby field.

_____

▢ ▢ ▢

Tuesday 8

Complete the analogy.

1. evening : dusk :: morning : _____

Correct these sentences.

2. lie them dirty clothes on top of the washing machine

_____

3. gen gonzales didnt say nothing to his troops

_____

Use context clues to determine the meaning of the bolded word below.

4. The lighthouse **illuminated** a spot over a mile away making it possible to see the sinking

ship. _____

Fact or opinion?

5. Boys look better with short hair. _____

Wednesday 8

Correct these sentences.

1. the explorers search the island but they never found no hidden treasure

2. were studying the poem paul reveres ride in english class

Which word would come first in alphabetical order?

3. enormous   energy   enthusiasm   enough

Which word IS spelled correctly?

4. studyed   studeed   studied   studed

Circle the adjectives in this sentence.

5. Amy's exotic parakeet laid three tiny eggs in the nest.

Thursday 8

Name this part of a friendly letter.

1. Terrance _____

What do the words in this group have in common?

2. microscope   telescope   binoculars   spectacles

Correct these sentences.

3. they have scene rainbows in the sky many times during april

4. helen and her english friend phyllis took a trip together

What contraction is made from these two words?

5. I will _____

Name: _____

Friday 8

Read the following paragraph and decide if the underlined parts have a capitalization error, a punctuation error, a spelling error, or no mistake.

Born in 1897 <u>in Atchison Kansas, Amelia</u> Earhart grew up with an interest in faraway
                           1

places. She took <u>her first plaen ride</u> in 1920 and decided to become a pilot herself. She
                        2

bought herself a plane for her twenty-fifth <u>birthday. She flew</u> airplanes and set many
                                                    3

aviation <u>records, but she also</u> taught immigrants and wrote a book. Earhart was the first
              4

woman to fly <u>across the atlantic ocean alone.</u>
                      5

1. _____   4. _____

2. _____   5. _____

3. _____

Daily Language Review

Answer Key 8

Monday
1. His parents went to a Chinese restaurant to celebrate their anniversary.
2. Prof. W. C. Wilson and his wife were both born on January 16, 1965.
3. yes
4. no
5. noun

Tuesday
1. dawn
2. Lay those dirty clothes on top of the washing machine.
3. Gen. Gonzales didn't say anything to his troops.
4. Illuminated means lighted or lit.
5. Opinion

Wednesday
1. The explorers searched the island, but they never found any hidden treasure.
2. We're studying the poem "Paul Revere's Ride" in English class.
3. energy
4. studied
5. exotic, three, tiny

Thursday
1. signature
2. They are all used to see things more clearly.
3. They have seen rainbows in the sky many times during April.
4. Helen and her English friend Phyllis took a trip together.
5. I'll

Friday
1. punctuation
2. spelling
3. no mistake
4. no mistake
5. capitalization

Name: _____

Monday 9

Correct these sentences.

1. they herd thunder and seen lighting during the storm

_____

2. this hole house is won big mess

_____

Give another word that would belong in this group.

3. Asia   North America   Europe   Antarctica _____

What time of day does the following probably happen?
4. Tom grabbed his lunch money and library book and ran for the school bus.

_____

Which word is NOT spelled correctly?

5. quickest   tinyest   loneliest   happiest

☐   ☐   ☐

Name: _____

Tuesday 9

Write two words that rhyme with stare.

1. _____   _____

What is the correct way to divide these words into syllables?

2. umpire   _____

3. cousin   _____

Correct these sentences.

4. michelle margo and martin came to syds house for sunday dinner

_____

5. the hole basketball team are going for pizza after the game

_____

Correct these sentences.

1. can you come with my friends and i to central park

_____

2. is adam spending august at lake tahoe or is he staying home

_____

Is the underlined word a subject pronoun or an object pronoun?

3. The teacher ask Pete to share <u>his</u> story with the class. _____

Complete the analogy.

4. Kenya : Africa :: Brazil : _____

What reference source would you use to find the longitude and latitude of Calcutta, India?

5. _____

What is the correct abbreviation for tablespoon?

1. tsp.   tblsp.   tbsp.   TB.

Which words have the same sound as /f/ in fall?

2. enough   fragile   ghost   photograph

Correct these sentences.

3. were leaving for kansas city kansas on the 6 oclock train

_____

4. tammi shouted keep away from that broken bottle

_____

Synonyms or antonyms?

5. relative, kin _____

Friday 9

Combine the sentences to make one sentence.

1. I have an uncle.   His name is Frank.   He lives in Toledo, Ohio.

2. There was a big storm.   It was a snow storm.   School was closed because of the storm.

3. Grandmother has a garden.   Corn grows in her garden.   Beans grow in her garden.

4. There were ten bands.   The bands marched in the parade.
They played music as they marched.

5. The children sang in the program.   The children danced in the program.
Parents watched the children perform.

Answer Key 9

Monday
1. They heard thunder and saw lightning during the storm.
2. This whole house is one big mess!
3. South America, Australia, or Africa
4. in the morning before school begins
5. tinyest

Tuesday
1. Answers will vary.
2. um pire
3. cous in
4. Michelle, Margo, and Martin came to Syd's house for Sunday dinner.
5. The whole basketball team is going for pizza after the game.

Wednesday
1. Can you come with my friends and me to Central Park?
2. Is Adam spending August at Lake Tahoe, or is he staying home?
3. an object pronoun
4. South America
5. atlas

Thursday
1. tbsp.
2. enough   fragile   photograph
3. We're leaving for Kansas City, Kansas, on the 6 o'clock train.
4. Tammi shouted, "Keep away from that broken bottle!"
5. synonyms

Friday
Sentences may vary somewhat. Accept any reasonable sentence construction that contains all the information.
1. My Uncle Frank lives in Toledo, Ohio.
2. School was closed because of a big snow storm.
3. Grandmother grows corn and beans in her garden.
4. The ten bands played music as they marched in the parade.
5. The children sang and danced in the program as parents watched them perform.

Name: _____

Monday **10**

Correct these sentences.

1. the scariest story marcus ever red was sounds in the night by t c jones

_____

2. mr and mrs valdez has traveled to many countrys around the world

_____

Fact or fantasy?

3. Several planets in our solar system are surrounded by rings. _____

What two words make up the contraction?

4. they've _____

Choose the best word to complete the sentence.

5. That car is the _____ vehicle on the block.

a. nosier   b. noisy   c. noisiest   d. none of these

☐ ☐ ☐

Name: _____

Tuesday **10**

Write an opinion about this topic: immigrants

1. _____

If the guide words on a page are "sidewalk" and "silence," which word would NOT be on the page?

2. sierra   sign   sieve   simple   sigh

Correct these sentences.

3. willie said ill get me and you something to drink

_____

4. wow perry thats a great dive shout carmen

_____

Use this homophone pair in one sentence. (scene, seen)

5.

Wednesday 10

Correct these sentences.

1. take a bath brush youre teeth and then go to bed

_____

2. cary dont go nowhere but home after school

_____

What is the present tense of the verb thought?

3. _____

Declarative, interrogative, imperative, or exclamatory?

4. Don't walk on the clean floor with those dirty feet. _____

What is the following person's job?

5. In a short time Clarissa returned to the table with Mr. and Mrs. O'Brien's dinner order.

Thursday 10

Which word would come last in alphabetical order?

1. wrist   women   written   wrong   worst

Give the plural of each noun.

2. roof _____   calf _____

Correct these sentences.

3. im going to the beach next weak announced tonya

_____

4. wasnt that the correct answer to harolds question

_____

Give the complete predicate of this sentence.

5. The outcome of the game depends on us.

_____

What do the underlined phrases mean?

1. Coach said the team was <u>driving him up the wall</u>.

2. Can you think of a way to get out of the <u>jam</u> you're in?

3. "<u>Don't bite my head off</u>," said Jules. "It wasn't my fault you got caught."

4. Why are you so <u>crazy about</u> that singer?

5. <u>You could have knocked me over with a feather</u> when he said that.

Daily Language Review

Answer Key 10

Monday
1. The scariest story Marcus ever read was <u>Sounds in the Night</u> by T. C. Jones.
2. Mr. and Mrs. Valdez have traveled to many countries around the world.
3. fact
4. they have
5. c. noisiest

Tuesday
1. Answers will vary.
2. simple
3. Willie said, "I'll get you and me something to drink."
4. "Wow, Perry, that's a great dive!" shouted Carmen.
5. Answers will vary.

Wednesday
1. Take a bath, brush your teeth, and then go to bed.
2. Cary doesn't go anywhere but home after school.
3. think
4. imperative
5. waitress, waitperson

Thursday
1. wrong
2. roofs   calves
3. "I'm going to the beach next week," announced Tonya.
4. Wasn't that the correct answer to Harold's question?
5. depends on us

Friday
1. bothering him; irritating him
2. predicament; difficult situation
3. don't speak so angrily at me
4. like a great deal; really admire
5. was very surprised

Correct these sentences.

1. wow what a great surprise shouted ernesto

_____

2. we dont want nobody to here our secret

_____

Add a suffix to this word.

3. care _____

Simile or metaphor?

4. Jeffrey was a <u>walking dictionary</u>. _____

Give another word that would belong in this group.

5. kiwi   guava   mango   pineapple

_____

Circle the words that rhyme.

1. joke mope cloak stake broke

2. away spry eight betray sleigh

Correct these sentences.

3. after working for two ours they was covered with dirt

_____

4. did your sister promised to arrive bye 6 pm for the party

_____

Name this part of a friendly letter.

5. I went to a soccer game with my friends Friday afternoon.

_____

Wednesday 11

Correct these sentences.

1. michael and me was excited about running in the boston marathon

2. i can sea hank that your studying hard

Which words have four syllables?

3. amphibian   motorcycle   frequency   semicircle

Circle the cause and underline the effect.

4. Tony was too big for his old bike, so he sold it at the flea market.

Give a common noun for each proper noun.

5. Mrs. Hernandez _____ San Francisco _____

Thursday 11

Give the comparative and superlative adjectives for lazy.

1. _____

Synonyms, antonyms, or homophones?

2. currency, money _____

Correct these sentences.

3. them storys mr feinstein told was really scary

4. have you ever went water skiing on lake michigan

The /ou/ in house sounds most like the vowel sound in:

5. enough   surround   cough   young

Friday 11

Choose the best word to complete each sentence.

1. The _____ of a skunk is very powerful.

   sent   cent   scent

2. How much _____ did your company make last year?

   profit   prophet   production

3. Her Saint Bernard puppy already _____ fifty pounds.

   waits   ways   weighs

4. How many _____ were sitting in the doctor's waiting room?

   patience   patients   patrons

5. Our tickets are for row "E" down that _____.

   isle   aisle   I'll

   ☐   ☐   ☐

Daily Language Review

Answer Key 11

Monday
1. "Wow, what a great surprise!" shouted Ernesto.
2. We don't want anybody to hear our secret.
3. careful, careless
4. metaphor
5. Answers will vary, but must be a fruit.

Tuesday
1. joke, cloak, broke
2. away, betray, sleigh
3. After working for two hours, they were covered in dirt.
4. Did your sister promise to arrive by 6 p.m. for the party?
5. body

Wednesday
1. Michael and I were excited about running in the Boston Marathon.
2. I can see, Hank, that you're studying hard.
3. amphibian, motorcycle, semicircle
4. Tony was too big for his old bike so he sold it at the flea market.
5. woman or lady   city

Thursday
1. lazier   laziest
2. synonyms
3. Those stories Mr. Feinstein told were really scary.
4. Have you ever gone water skiing on Lake Michigan?
5. surround

Friday
1. scent
2. profit
3. weighs
4. patients
5. aisle

Name:

Monday 12

Correct these sentences.

1. lisa and me are going ice skating at rainbow rinks

2. in september me and him gots to start going to middle school

Use context clues to determine the meaning of the bolded word below.

3. The hunter killed several deer to have enough **venison** to feed his family during the long, cold winter.

Which word IS spelled correctly?

4. princupal   principal   prinsipal   prencipal

Circle the adjectives in this sentence.

5. The cranky old woman kept the boys' ball when it came over her fence.

Daily Language Review

Name:

Tuesday 12

Which part of speech is underlined in the following sentence?

1. Seth <u>has passed</u> everyone in the motorcycle race.

Correct these sentences.

2. our teacher mr toscano hasnt had the measles the mumps or the chicken pox

3. why did me and her promise to clean up after the class party muttered kevin

Circle the preposition in this sentence.

4. The doctor stood beside his patient's bed.

Give an antonym for this word.

5. deceased _____

Wednesday 12

Correct these sentences.

1. dont weight until its to late to by an ticket for the show

2. why aint you got no time to help me

Complete the analogy.

3. horse : quadruped :: human : _____

Choose the best word to complete this sentence.

4. _____ that woman standing by your car?

Whose   Whom   Who's   Who

Circle the adverb in this sentence.

5. They are always late to ball games.

Thursday 12

Fact or opinion?

1. Oatmeal is delicious with milk and brown sugar.

Are the underlined words a common noun or a proper noun?

2. Margo and Beth went to an <u>amusement park</u> yesterday.

Correct these sentences.

3. theyre dinner reservation at kates kitchen is for 530 pm

4. the presidents guards has to be strong intelligent and reliable

Give a synonym for attempt.

5.

Friday 12

Which reference source would be best to look up the information: thesaurus, dictionary, telephone book, atlas, encyclopedia, or almanac?

1. what part of speech the word "really" is

2. the inventor of the steam engine

3. what the root word "auto" means

4. where to find the nearest Buddhist temple

5. the names of the Great Lakes

Answer Key 12

Monday
1. Lisa and I are going ice skating at Rainbow Rinks.
2. In September he and I have to start going to middle school.
3. Venison is deer meat.
4. principal
5. cranky, old

Tuesday
1. verb
2. Our teacher, Mr. Toscano, hasn't had the measles, the mumps, or the chicken pox.
3. "Why did she and I promise to clean up after the class party?" muttered Kevin.
4. beside
5. alive, living

Wednesday
1. Don't wait until it's too late to buy a ticket for the show.
2. Why don't you have any time to help me?
3. biped
4. Who's
5. always

Thursday
1. opinion
2. a common noun
3. Their dinner reservation at Kate's Kitchen is for 5:30 p.m.
4. The president's guards have to be strong, intelligent, and reliable.
5. try

Friday
1. dictionary
2. encyclopedia
3. dictionary
4. telephone book
5. atlas, encyclopedia

Monday **13**

Correct these sentences.

1. shannon done the cooking an cleaning while her mother was ill

_____

2. those is petes favorite music tapes

_____

Circle the adverb in this sentence.

3. We are going fishing tomorrow.

Choose the best word to complete this sentence.

4. Do you know Juan very _____ ?

   a. good   b. long   c. well   d. none of these

Divide this word into syllables.

5. generous   ☐ ☐ ☐

Tuesday **13**

Which word has the sound of /ch/ in cherry?

1. mention   future   school   bridge

Subject or predicate?

2. The doctor <u>observed the patient's reaction</u>.   _____

Correct these sentences.

3. did you sale on mr browns boat last weekend

_____

4. both boys bikes was read with black stripes

_____

Fact or opinion?

5. Eating vegetables can help you become a healthier person. _____

Wednesday 13

Correct these sentences.

1. jamal has done gone to visit his uncle in jacksonville illinois

_____

2. she yelled too warn him but it was to late

_____

Complete the analogy.

3. qt. : quart :: oz. : _____

Which word is NOT spelled correctly?

4. though   throat   thawt   through

Give the pronoun that would replace the underlined noun.

5. The <u>team</u> began to play at 3:00. _____

☐ ☐ ☐

Thursday 13

What contraction is made from these two words?

1. we have _____

What reference source would you use to find information about Thomas Edison's inventions?

2. _____

Correct these sentences.

3. father said nobody is going nowhere until our chores is done

_____

4. they aint played ice hockey since their goalie breaked his ankle

_____

Give a synonym for perhaps.

5. _____

Read the following paragraph and decide if the underlined parts have a capitalization error, a punctuation error, a spelling error, or no mistake.

<u>My aunt gertie likes to try</u> new things. Not <u>only dus she want</u> to try <u>new things, she wants you</u>
 1   **2**   **3**

to try them too. When you see her with <u>a big girn on her face,</u> you know something is
           4

about to happen. Pretty soon she is <u>saying, "let's</u> have an adventure."
          5

1. _____

2. _____

3. _____

4. _____

5. _____

Monday 14

Correct these sentences.

1. mervins dog wags its tale when it gets a bone

_____

2. bills baby sister torn the library books pages

_____

Use context clues to determine the meaning of the bolded word below.

3. The storm left Ralph **marooned** in his car on a lonely road until help could arrive.

_____

Give the past tense of these verbs.

4. wind _____

5. sweep _____

Tuesday 14

Give the plural noun.

1. octopus _____

Choose the best word to complete the sentence.

2. I wear _____ raincoat and take _____ umbrella with me when it rains.

      a   an   a   an

Correct these sentences.

3. me and him wanted to see the knew exhibit at sea world aquarium

_____

4. why dont he play quiet while the baby is napping

_____

Give the comparative and superlative adjectives.

5. pretty _____ _____

Correct these sentences.

1. mrs kotter said dont do that no more

2. did the womens lunches all costed the same amount

What is the base or root word?

3. population

What is the meaning of this figure of speech?

4. When I won the trophy you could have <u>knocked me over with a feather</u>.

Give the complete subject of this sentence.

5. The center of a tornado can cause a great deal of damage.

Subject pronoun or object pronoun?

1. Mom took Kim and <u>me</u> to the movies.

What part of speech is underlined in this sentence?

2. Annie waited <u>patiently</u> for her turn.

Correct these sentences.

3. for white swams swimmed around the large peaceful pond

4. peter paul and mary was having fun at abbies halloween party

Identify this part of a business letter.

5. Mr. T. E. Jones
   Kelly Toy Company
   1120 West Harding Street
   Memphis, TN 36123

Friday 14

Combine the sentences to make one sentence.

1. My friends were hungry.   They went into the kitchen.   They hunted for food.

2. Busy workers painted the house.   They painted the whole house.   It took one day.

3. Ernest fell down.   He scraped his knee.   Mother put a bandage on it.

4. Stacy had a crack in her tooth.   She went to the dentist.   The dentist fixed the crack.

5. The music store was having a sale.   Everything was 30% off.   I bought a saxophone.

Answer Key 14

Monday
1. Mervin's dog wags its tail when it gets a bone.
2. Bill's baby sister tore the library book's pages.
3. Marooned means stranded or left in a deserted place.
4. wound
5. swept

Tuesday
1. octopi, octopuses
2. a   an
3. He and I wanted to see the new exhibit at Sea World Aquarium.
4. Why doesn't he play quietly while the baby is napping?
5. prettier   prettiest

Wednesday
1. Mrs. Kotter said, "Don't do that any more."
2. Did the women's lunches all cost the same amount?
3. populate
4. It means being very surprised about what has occurred.
5. The center of a tornado

Thursday
1. object pronoun
2. adverb
3. Four white swams swam around the large, peaceful pond.
4. Peter, Paul, and Mary were having fun at Abbie's Halloween party.
5. heading

Friday
Sentences may vary somewhat. Accept any reasonable sentence construction that contains all the information.
1. My hungry friends went into the kitchen and hunted for food.
2. Busy workers painted the whole house in one day.
3. After Ernest fell down, Mother put a bandage on his scraped knee.
4. Stacy went to the dentist, and he fixed the crack in her tooth.
5. The music store was having a 30% off sale, so I bought a saxophone.

Name: _____

Monday 15

Correct these sentences.

1. did them special packages prof chang ordered arrive safely

_____

2. they was hungry and tired after helping jessie and i build a treehouse

_____

Identify the preposition in this sentence.

3. Marcos went swimming with his best friend. _____

Simile or metaphor?

4. She dressed <u>quick as a wink</u> and hurried off to her appointment. _____

Which words are NOT spelled correctly?

5. ecology   histry   energy   apolugy   mystery

               ☐   ☐   ☐

Name: _____

Tuesday 15

Complete the analogy.

1. shark : fish :: koala : _____

What is the correct abbreviation for pound?

2. pd.   P.   LB   lb.

Correct these sentences.

3. theys not taking class pictures until wednesday at 145

_____

4. you cant make me do nothing i dont want to do yelled mitchell

_____

Past, present, or future?

5. leapt _____

Name: _____

Wednesday 15

Correct these sentences.

1. that greedy little child drinked all the cold lemonade they done had

_____

2. terrys brothers afraid of the dark so mom gived him a flashlight

_____

What do the words in this group have in common?

3. pencil   pen   typewriter   computer

_____

If the guide words on a page are "laundry" and "lawn," which words would NOT be on the page?

4. lavender   lawyer   lax   lava   lavish

Does the underlined adverb tell how, when, where, or to what extent?

5. It is <u>always</u> fun to visit Aunt Eloise.

☐   ☐   ☐

Name: _____

Thursday 15

Does this word have a prefix or a suffix?

1. misunderstood   _____

Give the singular form for this plural noun.

2. knives   _____

Correct these sentences.

3. alice who lived next door goed to a different school

_____

4. stopping by woods on a snowy evening by robert frost is my mothers favorite poem

_____

Synonyms or antonyms?

5. group, individual   _____

Name: _____

Friday 15

What do the underlined phrases mean?

1. It has been <u>raining cats and dogs</u> all day.

_____

2. Paolo's teacher was <u>singing his praises</u> when she met his parents.

_____

3. "<u>Don't count your chickens before they hatch</u>," he warned the children.

_____

4. She crept <u>quiet as a mouse</u> past the baby's crib.

_____

5. It turned out to be a <u>wild goose chase</u> after all.

_____

Daily Language Review

Answer Key 15

Monday
1. Did those special packages Prof. Chang ordered arrive safely?
2. They were hungry and tired after helping Jessie and me build a treehouse.
3. with
4. simile
5. histry, apolugy

Tuesday
1. marsupial
2. lb.
3. They're not taking class pictures until Wednesday at 1:45.
4. "You can't make me do anything I don't want to do!" yelled Mitchell.
5. past

Wednesday
1. That greedy, little child drank all the cold lemonade they had.
2. Terry's brother's afraid of the dark, so his mom gave him a flashlight.

3. They are all used to record information, thoughts, etc.
4. lawyer, lax
5. to what extent

Thursday
1. prefix
2. knife
3. Alice, who lived next door, went to a different school.
4. "Stopping by Woods on a Snowy Evening" by Robert Frost is my mother's favorite poem.
5. antonyms

Friday
1. very heavy rainfall
2. saying nice things
3. don't count on the result until it happens; don't spend your money before you get it
4. made no noise at all; very quiet
5. a lot of effort with no result; looking for something that was never there

Correct these sentences.

1. sammy please hand me them pliers said the instructor

2. its obvious you dont have no money to lend me

Circle the cause and underline the effect.

3. When the baseball hit the front window, one pane of glass was broken.

Identify where the colon is used correctly.

4. aren:t   11:00   Dear Uncle Jim: Sincerely:

Use this homophone pair in one sentence. (aloud, allowed)

5.

If the guide words on a page were "pause" and "payment," which words would be on the page?

1. payroll   pattern   patriot   pavilion   peacock

Correct these sentences.

2. it don't make no difference since my mom wont let me go with you

3. dr otis scolded you should of been more careful

What is the root or base word?

4. prehistory

Give the plural form of this noun.

5. latch

Wednesday 16

Correct these sentences.

1. she has swam the english channel several times in the passed year

2. why did them mooses cross the river so near roberts cabin

Declarative, interrogative, imperative, or exclamatory?

3. Put your dirty clothes in the hamper.

Subject pronoun or object pronoun?

4. <u>They</u> jogged three miles everyday for a month.

Which words have three syllables?

5. government   fragment   amusement   predicament

Thursday 16

Which reference source would you use to find out how many inches of rain fell in Oklahoma in 1996?

1.

Fiction or nonfiction?

2. Frozen drops of water fell from the sky covering everything in a blanket of white.

Correct these sentences.

3. the bishops asked margaret to sing the anniversary waltz at their celebration

4. carlos has did his work correct

Which part of speech is underlined?

5. Will you get warts if you pick up a <u>bumpy</u> toad?

Name: _____

Friday 16

Choose the best word to complete each sentence.

1. If we play _____ at the audition, we may be hired.
   well   good   best

2. Did you have a _____ time on your vacation in Spain?
   well   good   best

3. _____ apricots are the best I've ever tasted.
   Them   Those   That

4. Please help _____ fix the flat tire.
   she   her   I

5. Margo and _____ have signed up for ballet lessons.
   her   I   us

Daily Language Review

Answer Key 16

Monday
1. "Sammy, please hand me those pliers," said the instructor.
2. It's obvious you don't have any money to lend me.
3. When (the baseball hit the front window,) one pane of glass was broken.
4. 11:00
5. Answers will vary.

Tuesday
1. pavilion
2. It doesn't make any difference, since my mom won't let me go with you.
3. Dr. Otis scolded, "You should have been more careful."
4. history
5. latches

Wednesday
1. She has swum the English Channel several times in the past year.
2. Why did those moose cross the river so near Robert's cabin?
3. imperative
4. subject pronoun
5. government   amusement

Thursday
1. almanac
2. nonfiction
3. The Bishops asked Margaret to sing "The Anniversary Waltz" at their celebration.
4. Carlos has done his work correctly.
5. adjective

Friday
1. well
2. good
3. Those
4. her
5. I

Monday 17

Correct these sentences.

1. his favorite poem is stuarts worst nightmare

2. my brother and me need to bye shirts pants socks and shoes for school

Is part of the subject or part of the predicate underlined?

3. <u>Was</u> Herbert <u>cleaning</u> his messy room?

Punctuate this address.

4. 326 West 18th St

   Seattle WA 96430

Give an opinion about this topic: extraterrestrial life forms

5.

Tuesday 17

What two words make up this contraction?

1. who'll

Synonyms or antonyms?

2. allow, prohibit

Correct these sentences.

3. during the rainy season in africa rain falls everyday

4. the main street school team were the best in the area

Find the prepositional phrase in the sentence.

5. Water flowed under the covered bridge.

Name:

Wednesday [17]

Correct these sentences.

1. when will the technician ms rawlings fix hour computer

_____

2. the dogs tails wagged as father gave them johns leftovers

_____

Complete the analogy.

3. square : plane :: cube : _____

Choose the best word to complete this sentence.

4. He _____ his glasses on the night stand when he goes to bed.

    sit   set   sits   sets

Use this homophone pair in one sentence. (piece, peace)

5. _____

☐ ☐ ☐

Name:

Thursday [17]

Which word is NOT spelled correctly?

1. surely   usully   several   loose

Proper noun or common noun?

2. Kentucky   _____

3. skateboard   _____

Correct these sentences.

4. have you ever red popular mechanics asked orlando

_____

5. they all singed happy birthday before her cut the cake

_____

Which reference source would be best to look up the information: thesaurus, dictionary, telephone book, atlas, encyclopedia, or almanac?

1. the names of several gardeners in your area

2. what a sloth eats

3. what direction you would travel from Botswana to Pakistan

4. an antonym for "complex"

5. the average temperature of Memphis, Tennessee, in May

Daily Language Review

Answer Key **17**

Monday
1. His favorite poem is "Stuart's Worst Nightmare."
2. My brother and I need to buy shirts, pants, socks, and shoes for school.
3. predicate
4. 326 West 18th St.
   Seattle, WA 96430
5. Answers will vary.

Tuesday
1. who will
2. antonyms
3. During the rainy season in Africa, rain falls every day.
4. The Main Street School team was the best in the area.
5. under the covered bridge

Wednesday
1. When will the technician, Ms. Rawlings, fix our computer?
2. The dogs' tails wagged as Father gave them John's leftovers.
3. solid
4. sets
5. Answers will vary.

Thursday
1. usully
2. proper noun
3. common noun
4. "Have you ever read Popular Mechanics?" asked Orlando.
5. They all sang "Happy Birthday" before she cut the cake.

Friday
1. telephone book
2. encyclopedia
3. atlas
4. thesaurus
5. almanac

Name: _____

Monday 18

Correct these sentences.

1. can jan and me stay overnight at aunt marys

_____

2. them noisy children yelled loud as they played outside

_____

Use context clues to determine the meaning of the bolded word below.

3. Your headache may go away if you **recline** on the sofa and close your eyes.

_____

Choose the word that best completes this sentence.

4. The pitcher _____ the ball across the plate striking out the batter.
   a. throwed   b. through   c. threw   d. none of these

If the guide words on a page were "ample" and "anchor," which word would be on the page?

5. anvil   amber   ancient   amusement   amaze

☐   ☐   ☐

Name: _____

Tuesday 18

What is the correct contraction for of the clock?

1. _____

Use this homophone pair in one sentence. (I'll, aisle)

2. _____

Correct these sentences.

3. the farmers oxes was held together by a wooden yolk

_____

4. throughout the long stormy night the excited campers shared ghost storys

_____

Identify this part of a business letter.

5. Dear Mr. President: _____

Wednesday 18

Correct these sentences.

1. the diver exclaimed i never done no dive like that before

_____

2. youll need clay glaze and a kiln to make an ceramic vase

_____

Subject pronoun or object pronoun?

3. Is <u>he</u> ready to go? _____

Fact or fiction?

4. An ancient species of dragon was found living in Antarctica. _____

Do the underlined adjectives tell which one, what kind, or how many?

5. The <u>hungry</u> robins were looking for <u>juicy</u> worms to eat.

☐   ☐   ☐

Thursday 18

Is the underlined word a common noun or a proper noun?
1. The <u>captain</u> of the Enterprise ordered the crew to abandon ship. _____

What type of sentence is this?

2. Have you ever been sent to the principal's office. _____

Correct these sentences.

3. are you gonna go mountain climbing with theyre group

_____

4. him and me took a guitar lesson thursday at 430

_____

Synonyms, antonyms, or homophones?

5. kernel, colonel _____

Read the following paragraph and decide if the underlined parts have a capitalization error, a punctuation error, a spelling error, or no mistake.

Washing machines used to be run by <u>human power. hot water was</u> poured into a tub,
                                          1

dirty clothes were rubbed <u>with a bar of soap, and them</u> scrubbed against <u>a bored with ridges</u>,
                              2   **3**

called a washboard. After a second dipping into <u>clean water the clothes were</u> twisted to get
                                                    4

the water <u>out and hung</u> on a line to dry.
              5

1. _____   4. _____

2. _____   5. _____

3. _____

Daily Language Review

Answer Key 18

Monday
1. Can Jan and I stay overnight at Aunt Mary's?
2. Those noisy children yelled loudly as they played outside.
3. Recline means to lean backwards or lie down.
4. c. threw
5. amusement

Tuesday
1. o'clock
2. Answers will vary.
3. The farmer's oxen were held together by a wooden yoke.
4. Throughout the long, stormy night, the excited campers shared ghost stories.
5. Salutation

Wednesday
1. The diver exclaimed, "I never did a dive like that before!"
2. You'll need clay, glaze, and a kiln to make a ceramic vase.
3. subject pronoun
4. fiction
5. what kind

Thursday
1. common noun
2. interrogative
3. Are you going to go mountain climbing with their group?
4. He and I took a guitar lesson Thursday at 4:30.
5. homophones

Friday
1. capitalization
2. spelling
3. spelling
4. punctuation
5. no mistake

Say "Said" Sixty Ways

Sample Passage A

"What do you want to do today?" said Sam.

"I don't know. Maybe we can go rollerblading in the park," said Ceil.

"I hate rollerblading," said Sam.

"Okay, so what do you want today?" said Ceil.

Sample Passage B

"What do you want to do today?" asked Sam.

"I don't know. Maybe we can go rollerblading in the park," suggested Ceil.

"I hate rollerblading," muttered Sam.

"Okay, so what do you want to do today?" retorted Ceil.

Why is it more effective to use a variety of words instead of using the word *said*?

_____

_____

_____

_____

EN

Say "Said" Sixty Ways *(cont.)*

wondered	bothered	quibbled
thought	fretted	bickered
mouthed	fussed	squabbled
whispered	mimicked	retorted
muttered	teased	disputed
murmured	joked	debated
evaded	jested	opposed
remarked	struggled	sputtered
mentioned	suggested	reacted
stated	speculated	spat
uttered	guessed	argued
spoke	asked	quarreled
bade	requested	lashed
voiced	queried	yelled
explained	answered	shouted
accounted	responded	screamed
decided	replied	exploded
determined	chimed	screeched
chose	applauded	whined
concocted	approved	mused
worried	decreed	

58

Correct these sentences.

1. the man next door never goed too no partys

_____

2. i cant never decide which i like best is halloween or valentines day the most fun

_____

Does the underlined adverb tell how, when, where, or to what extent?

3. Chocolate milk flew <u>everywhere</u> when the carton broke. _____

Choose the best word to complete the sentence.

4. Bob ate _____ pieces of chicken than Curtis.
   few   less   fewer   lesser

What is the correct way to divide this word into syllables?

5. physi i cian   phy si cian   phy si ci an

   ☐   ☐   ☐

Complete the analogy.

1. emu : bird :: frog : _____

Which word does not belong in this group?

2. wolf   giraffe   chicken   lizard   toad

Correct these sentences.

3. grandmother taked my brother and me to buy candles for hour kwanzaa celebration

_____

4. after the bean seed sprouted it growed three inches in a weak

_____

Declarative, interrogative, imperative, or exclamatory?

5. Our last adventure together was a trip to the Hawaiian Islands _____

Name: _____

Wednesday 19

Correct these sentences.

1. get them dirty dogs off of my clean sofa shouted nana

_____

2. why do this pie have less peaces than the others

_____

Give the past tense of the verb satisfy.

3. _____

Singular possessive or plural possessive?

4. Carlos's bike _____

5. the ladies' club _____

Name: _____

Thursday 19

Add a prefix to this word.

1. appear _____

Where would the following probably take place?

2. "That will be $6.59. Pick up your order at the window."

_____

Correct these sentences.

3. them terrible winds blew a umbrella and a picnic table threw our front window

_____

4. yoko tells real funny jokes and she makes silly faces to

_____

What word IS spelled correctly?

5. broaken   stranje   straight   hungery

Name:

Friday 19

Combine the sentences to make one sentence.

1. The cookie jar was empty.   Mother made a batch of cookies.   She put the cookies in the jar.

2. Our teacher read us three stories.   They were funny stories.   She read them to us today.

3. We wandered along the crowded wharf.   We watched the tall ships. The ships sail into the harbor.

4. One hot day we bought ice cream cones.   We sat in the shade of a tree. We ate our ice cream cones.

5. The children watched the ball game.   They traded baseball cards. They talked about the players.

Answer Key 19

Monday
1. The man next door never went to any parties.
2. I can't ever decide which I like best. Is Halloween or Valentine's Day the most fun?
3. where
4. fewer
5. phy si cian

Tuesday
1. amphibian
2. chicken - It has only two legs; the others have four legs.
3. Grandmother took my brother and me to buy candles for our Kwanzaa celebration.
4. After the bean seed sprouted, it grew three inches in a week.
5. declarative

Wednesday
1. "Get those dirty dogs off my clean sofa!" shouted Nana.
2. Why does this pie have fewer pieces than the others?
3. satisfied
4. singular possessive
5. plural possessive

Thursday
1. reappear, disappear
2. fast-food restaurant; drive-through restaurant
3. Those terrible winds blew an umbrella and a picnic table through our front window.
4. Yoko tells really funny jokes, and she makes silly faces too.
5. straight

Friday
Sentences may vary somewhat. Accept any reasonable sentence construction that contains all the information.
1. Mother made a batch of cookies and put them in the empty cookie jar.
2. Our teacher read us three funny stories today.
3. We wandered along the crowded wharf watching the tall ships sail into the harbor.
4. One hot day we bought ice cream cones and sat in the shade of a tree to eat them.
5. The children watched the ball game, traded baseball cards, and talked about the players.

         Daily Language Review Grade 5 EMC 583

Monday 20

Correct these sentences.

1. during his trip to the zoo paul observed the monkeys apes and chimpanzees

2. does they want to come to aerobics class with shawn and i

What part of speech is the underlined word in this sentence?

3. The hailstones pounded the roof <u>during</u> the storm.

Give the plural noun for this singular noun.

4. blueberry

Identify where the apostrophe is NOT used correctly.

5. can't   has'nt   they've   it's

☐   ☐   ☐

Tuesday 20

Which word is NOT spelled correctly?
1. calender   dollar   visitor   thirsty

Correct these sentences.
2. the play was very good because them actors performed sew good

3. aunt gertie rushed in shouting lets have a adventure

Use context clues to determine the meaning of the bolded word below.
4. The driver was seriously injured when his car went out of control and plunged down a 100-foot **precipice**.

Simile or metaphor?
5. His new cousin was <u>cute as a bug in a rug</u>.

Wednesday 20

Correct these sentences.

1. did you no the colorado river run through the grand canyon

_____

2. mrs arnold my third grade teacher read us charlotte's web

_____

What reference source would you use to find the capital of China?

3. _____

What is the meaning of the abbreviation mph?

4. _____

Circle the cause and underline the effect.

5. Bernie's diligent practice paid off when he won the trophy.

☐ ☐ ☐

Daily Language Review
Name:

Thursday 20

Which word would come last in alphabetical order?

1. chinese   change   chocolate   challenge   champion

Give a homophone for paws.

2. _____

Correct these sentences.

3. well you certainly done a good job on youre science report

_____

4. the rich tropical rainforests of brazil is disappearing

_____

Which words are adverbs?

5. very   here   flew   gently

Name:

Friday 20

What do the underlined phrases mean?

1. I want to learn the whole poem <u>by heart</u>.

2. Toby was <u>green with envy</u> when his best friend's project won first place in the science fair.

3. They looked like <u>two peas in a pod</u> in their Halloween costumes.

4. I'm afraid I may be <u>in over my head</u> with this job.

5. Listening to his report was <u>as interesting as watching paint dry</u>.

Daily Language Review

Answer Key 20

Monday
1. During his trip to the zoo, Paul observed the monkeys, apes, and chimpanzees.
2. Do they want to come to aerobics class with Shawn and me?
3. preposition
4. blueberries
5. has'nt

Tuesday
1. calendar
2. The play was very good because those actors performed so well.
3. Aunt Gertie rushed in shouting, "Let's have an adventure!"
4. A precipice is a cliff with a very steep slope.
5. simile

Wednesday
1. Did you know the Colorado River runs through the Grand Canyon?
2. Mrs. Arnold, my third grade teacher, read us <u>Charlotte's Web</u>.

3. atlas, encyclopedia, almanac
4. miles per hour
5. Bernie's diligent practice paid off when <u>he won the trophy</u>.

Thursday
1. chocolate
2. pause
3. Well, you certainly did a good job on your science report.
4. The rich, tropical rainforests of Brazil are disappearing.
5. very, here, gently

Friday
1. from memory
2. jealous
3. just alike; identical
4. the job is too difficult for me to do
5. boring

Monday 21

Correct these sentences.

1. matt walked nervous to the plate knowing his team would loose the game if he striked out

2. boy we was sure tired after climbing to the top of pikes peak

Circle the cause and underline the effect.

3. Bob rubbed his aching back and thought, "I'll never forget my air mattress again when I go camping overnight!"

Give two words that rhyme with the following word.

4. please

Circle the antonyms in this sentence.

5. Mr. Bradshaw has an enormous Saint Bernard and a minuscule Chihuahua as pets.

Tuesday 21

Choose the word that best completes the sentence.

1. The surface of the pond _____ over night.
   freeze   freezed   frozen   froze

Which words have the same sound as /ow/ in now?

2. bough   country   council   chowder   bowl

Correct these sentences.

3. sherry need a new break on her motorcycle before shell be able to race

4. theys dog gots mud in his fir from rolling in a mud puddle

Fact or fantasy?

5. Astronomers say there will be a shower of falling stars next Friday night.

Wednesday 21

Correct these sentences.

1. them kids all choosed hatchet as theyre favorite literature book

2. anita dont know how to play the star spangled banner yet

What is the present tense of the verb brought?

3.

If the guide words on a page are "crochet" and "crossbones," which words would NOT be on the page?

4. criticize   crocodile   croquet   crouch   crocus

Complete the analogy.

5. tsunami : water :: cyclone :

Thursday 21

Subject pronoun or object pronoun?

1. Uncle Fred bought <u>us</u> pizza.

Where is someone who is hearing the following?

2. "You must be at least ten years old and five feet tall to go on this ride."

Correct these sentences.

3. after he gived his dog a bath carlos was so wet and dirty he taked one hisself

4. why doesnt you come over four homemade ice cream said mr choi

What is the root or base word?

5. disappointment

Friday 21

Choose the best word to complete each sentence.

1. When _____ you need to catch the bus?

    does   do   was   is

2. My parents _____ married in 1980.

    was   were   been   did

3. Conrad, please give a cup of coffee to _____.

    he   they   him   I

4. How many baby _____ were born last night?

    bunnys   bunny's   bunnies   bunnies'

5. _____ going fishing with you?

    Whose   Who's   Who   Whom

Daily Language Review

Answer Key 21

Monday
1. Matt walked nervously to the plate knowing his team would lose the game if he struck out.
2. Boy, we were sure tired after climbing to the top of Pike's Peak.
3. Bob rubbed his aching back and thought, "I'll never forget my air mattress again when I go camping overnight!"
4. Answers will vary.
5. enormous, minuscule

Tuesday
1. froze
2. bough   council   chowder
3. Sherry needs a new brake on her motorcycle before she'll be able to race.
4. Their dog has mud in his fur from rolling in a mud puddle.
5. fact

Wednesday
1. Those kids all chose Hatchet as their favorite literature book.
2. Anita doesn't know how to play "The Star Spangled Banner" yet.
3. bring
4. criticize, crouch
5. wind, air

Thursday
1. object pronoun
2. in line for an amusement park ride
3. After he gave his dog a bath, Carlos was so wet and dirty he took one himself.
4. "Why don't you come over for homemade ice cream?" said Mr. Choi.
5. appoint

Friday
1. do
2. were
3. him
4. bunnies
5. who's

Monday | 22

Correct these sentences.

1. miguel pablo and carlotta is going to mexico for christmas

_____

2. dont walk threw them mud puddles in your good shoes

_____

Use context clues to determine the meaning of the underlined word.

3. That <u>tenacious</u> salesman just wouldn't take no for an answer.

_____

Which word IS spelled correctly?

4. tecknology   techology   technology   tecnology

Singular possessive or plural possessive?

5. Those <u>children's</u> parents are engineers.

☐   ☐   ☐

Tuesday | 22

Circle the adjectives in this sentence.

1. Several gray cats were napping in the warm sunshine.

Which word would come last in alphabetical order?

2. unicorn   unique   unicycle   uniform   union

Correct these sentences.

3. lets meat at the park four a picnic

_____

4. put that down write now and dont took it again

_____

Underline the prepositional phrase in the sentence.

5. The little children raced around the playground.

Wednesday 22

Correct these sentences.

1. if we leave now she said well be right on time

_____

2. do you have dear mr henshaw alice ask the clerk

_____

What is the correct abbreviation for boulevard?

3. BD   blvd.   boul.   bd.

Add a suffix to this word.

4. strange   _____

What is the subject of this sentence?

5. Will he be able to fix the broken television?

Thursday 22

Give synonyms for these words.

1. revolve   _____

2. thought   _____

Correct these sentences.

3. they got a serious problem can you helped them solve it

_____

4. im happy kenny to see youve cleaned up your mess

_____

Divide the following word into syllables.

5. transportation   _____

Name:

Friday  22

Which reference source would be best to look up the information: thesaurus, dictionary, telephone book, atlas, encyclopedia, or almanac?

1. information about invertebrates

2. the area code of Pacific Grove, CA

3. a synonym for "enchantment"

4. the capital city of Turkmenistan

5. the childhood of President Woodrow Wilson

Answer Key 22

Monday
1. Miguel, Pablo, and Carlotta are going to Mexico for Christmas.
2. Don't walk through those mud puddles in your good shoes.
3. persistent, won't give up
4. technology
5. plural possessive

Tuesday
1. several, gray, warm
2. unique
3. Let's meet at the park for a picnic.
4. Put that down right now, and don't take it again!
5. around the playground

Wednesday
1. "If we leave now," she said, "we'll be right on time."
2. "Do you have Dear Mr. Henshaw?" Alice asked the clerk.
3. blvd.
4. strangely, stranger, strangest
5. he

Thursday
1. twist, turn, rotate
2. idea, concept
3. They have a serious problem. Can you help them solve it?
4. I'm happy, Kenny, to see you've cleaned up your mess.
5. trans por ta tion

Friday
1. encyclopedia
2. telephone book
3. thesaurus
4. atlas, almanac, encyclopedia
5. encyclopedia

Monday 23

Correct these sentences.

1. im reading one chapter of tom sawyer every night before i go to bed

2. every saturday morning at 900 my little brother watches muppet babies

What is another word that belongs in this group?

3. tornado   thunderstorm   hurricane   blizzard

Past, present, or future?

4. Madge is planning to go to camp when school is out in June.

Name this part of a business letter.

5. The meeting should take no more than two hours.

Tuesday 23

Choose the best word to complete this sentence.

1. I'm so tired I think I'll _____ on the sofa and take a nap.
   lay   laid   lie   lying

If the guide words on a page were "armchair" and "arrange," which word would be on the page?

2. armadillo   arrow   arena   armor   arrest

Correct these sentences.

3. we read articles from newsweek time and the daily herald for are report

4. is the nile the longest river in africa garth wanted to no

Synonyms or antonyms?

5. polite, rude

Wednesday 23

Correct these sentences.

1. did you see the lost kingdom on television last knight

2. there was a large potwhole in the rode but i swerved and mist it

Write a fact about this topic: allowance

3. _____

Circle the synonyms in this sentence.

4. Misha's elderly aunt and her old cat live down the street.

Does the underlined adverb tell how, when, where, or to what extent?

5. It snowed for hours <u>yesterday</u>.

Thursday 23

Give the possessive noun.

1. the baby sister of Arturo

Use context clues to determine the meaning of the bolded word below.

2. My cat carried her kitten gently by the **nape** of its neck.

Correct these sentences.

3. dr roth our veterinarian told us to handle the hamster babys with care

4. is we supposed to read across the plains or mountain trek in our history books

Does the underlined adjective tell which one, what kind, or how many?

5. <u>That</u> kitten likes to chase the wind-up mouse.

Read the following paragraph and decide if the underlined parts have a capitalization error, a punctuation error, a spelling error, or no mistake.

Some people still think of <u>huge creatures when someone</u> mentions <u>dinosaurs? Well, they</u>
                             1   **2**

were not all big. <u>In fact compsognathus</u> was one of the smallest dinosaurs. It was about
                     3

the size of a <u>chicken, But its</u> small size wasn't a handicap. It was a swift and deadly
                     4

<u>hunter, using shrap teeth</u> and two-fingered hands to catch and hold prey.
        5

1. _____   4. _____

2. _____   5. _____

3. _____

Monday
1. I'm reading one chapter of <u>Tom Sawyer</u> every night before I go to bed.
2. Every Saturday morning at 9:00 my little brother watches <u>Muppet Babies</u>.
3. Answers will vary but must be a type of storm.
4. future
5. body

Tuesday
1. lie
2. armor
3. We read articles from <u>Newsweek</u>, <u>Time</u>, and <u>The Daily Herald</u> for our report.
4. "Is the Nile the longest river in Africa?" Garth wanted to know.
5. antonyms

Wednesday
1. Did you see <u>The Lost Kingdom</u> on television last night?
2. There was a large pothole in the road, but I swerved and missed it.
3. Answers will vary but must be factual.
4. elderly, old
5. when

Thursday
1. Arturo's baby sister
2. back of the neck
3. Dr. Roth, our veterinarian, told us to handle the hamster babies with care.
4. Are we supposed to read "Across the Plains" or "Mountain Trek" in our history books?
5. which one

Friday
1. no mistake
2. punctuation
3. punctuation
4. capitalization
5. spelling

Monday 24

Correct these sentences.

1. did you read the article called kayaking in alaska in geographic world magazine

_____

2. rev murphy their minister has worked in churches in australia guatemala and sri lanka

_____

Does the underlined adverb tell how, when, where, or to what extent?

3. The falling leaves flew <u>everywhere</u> in the park.

_____

Simile or metaphor?

4. I'm a <u>real chicken</u> when it comes to heights.

_____

Is the underlined noun singular or plural?

5. Which <u>person</u> do you feel gave the best speech?

☐ ☐ ☐

Tuesday 24

Subject pronoun or object pronoun?

1. <u>We</u> bought ice-cream cones for a snack.

_____

Correct these sentences.

2. angie said paul what is the answer to this riddle

_____

3. stans cat ollie clumb all over the furniture then he tryed to catch the goldfish

_____

What is the meaning of this figure of speech?

4. Everyone was upset with Larry after he <u>let the cat out of the bag</u> about the surprise party.

_____

Identify the subject of this sentence.

5. The natives of the tiny village celebrated with a great feast.

Wednesday 24

Correct these sentences.

1. if i put things away i wont be able to find anything complained herbert

2. very well said jose ill race you an i will win

Choose the best word to complete the sentence.

3. There are _____ many mistakes in this report.

two   to   too   tow

Where does the colon go?

4. 1230

5. Buy these at the store

☐   ☐   ☐

Thursday 24

Which contraction IS spelled correctly?

1. wel'l   they're   its'   does'nt

Which part of speech is underlined – noun, verb, adjective, or adverb?

2. Mother sang <u>softly</u> as she rocked the baby to sleep. _____

Correct these sentences.

3. millie red snow white and the seven dwarfs to her niece

4. peel the potatoes put them in a pot add water and cook them until they are soft

Synonyms or antonyms?

5. initial, final _____

Friday 24

Combine the sentences to make one sentence.

1. Mother received candy for her birthday.   The box was heart-shaped.   She was surprised.

   _____

2. Grandfather and I went camping at Bass Lake.   We slept in a tent.
   We cooked over a campfire.

   _____

3. There were icy patches on the sidewalk.   The man slipped on an icy patch.
   He broke his leg.

   _____

4. The boys played a board game.   It was Monopoly.   They played it for hours.

   _____

5. A tornado moved across the plains.   It touched down on our farm.
   It destroyed the barn.

   _____

Answer Key 24

Monday
1. Did you read the article called "Kayaking in Alaska" in <u>Geographic World</u> magazine?
2. Rev. Murphy, their minister, has worked in churches in Australia, Guatemala, and Sri Lanka.
3. where
4. metaphor
5. singular

Tuesday
1. subject pronoun
2. "Angie," said Paul, "what is the answer to this riddle?" OR
   Angie said, "Paul, what is the answer to this riddle?"
3. Stan's cat Ollie climbed all over the furniture. Then he tried to catch the goldfish.
4. Larry gave away the secret.
5. The natives of the tiny village

Wednesday
1. "If I put things away, I won't be able to find anything," complained Herbert.
2. "Very well," said Jose. "I'll race you and I will win!"
3. too
4. 12:30
5. Buy these at the store:

Thursday
1. they're
2. adverb
3. Millie read <u>Snow White and the Seven Dwarfs</u> to her niece.
4. Peel the potatoes, put them in a pot, add water, and cook them until they're soft.
5. antonyms

Friday
Sentences may vary somewhat. Accept any reasonable sentence construction that contains all the information.
1. Mother was surprised when she received a heart-shaped box of candy for her birthday.
2. Grandfather and I slept in a tent and cooked over a campfire when we went camping at Bass Lake.
3. The man broke his leg when he slipped on an icy patch on the sidewalk.
4. The boys played the board game Monopoly for hours.
5. A tornado moved across the plains destroying the barn when it touched down on our farm.

     Daily Language Review Grade 5 EMC 583

Name: _____

Monday [25]

Correct these sentences.

1. after it rang four times capt ruiz finally answered his phone

_____

2. hour trip will last from may 29 1998 until aug 29 1998

_____

Give the possessive noun.

3. the purses of the ladies _____

Use this homophone pair in one sentence. (rows, rose)

4. _____

Fact or opinion?

5. People should never pierce their ears. _____

☐ ☐ ☐

Name: _____

Tuesday [25]

Give the comparative and superlative forms of angry.

1. _____

Which part of speech is underlined – noun, verb, adjective, or adverb?

2. The <u>ancient</u> barn on Grandpa's farm is beginning to collapse.

_____

Correct the sentences.

3. after working for ate hours george and tyrone was exhausted

_____

4. dad taked both familys to pizza palace after the movie

_____

What is the correct way to divide the word into syllables?

5. re gu lar   reg u lar   reg ul ar   re gul ar

Wednesday 25

Correct these sentences.

1. to be successful you gotta work really hard

_____

2. ms thomas his secretary is on vacation in tampa florida

_____

Complete the analogy.

3. pachyderm : elephant :: crocodilian : _____

Suffix or prefix?

4. population   _____

5. disregard   _____

Thursday 25

Circle the cause and underline the effect.

1. Once the water begins to boil, Mother's teakettle whistles.

What reference source would you use to find an antonym for clever?

2. _____

Correct these sentences.

3. prof tanaka has forgot hes giving a lecture tomorrow at 830

_____

4. does your brothers get along very good

_____

Choose the correct date to complete the sentence.

5. I was born on _____ at Queen of Angels Hospital.
    May 20 1986   May 20, 1986,   May 20, 1986

Name:

Friday **25**

Write what the underlined phrases mean.

1. Dad was smiling <u>from ear to ear</u> as he held the new baby.

2. <u>Time stood still</u> as we waited to hear the winner's name.

3. "<u>Stop bugging me</u>!" he shouted at his little sister.

4. It must be true, <u>I got it straight from the horse's mouth</u>.

5. His boss just <u>gave him the ax</u>.

Answer Key **25**

Monday
1. After it rang four times, Capt. Ruiz finally answered his phone.
2. Our trip will last from May 29, 1998, until Aug. 29, 1998.
3. the ladies' purses
4. Answers will vary.
5. opinion

Tuesday
1. angrier, angriest
2. adjective
3. After working for eight hours, George and Tyrone were exhausted.
4. Dad took both families to Pizza Palace after the movie.
5. reg u lar

Wednesday
1. To be successful, you have to work really hard.
2. Ms. Thomas, his secretary, is on vacation in Tampa, Florida.
3. crocodile, alligator, or caimin
4. suffix
5. prefix

Thursday
1. Once the water begins to boil, Mother's <u>teakettle whistles</u>.
2. thesaurus
3. Prof. Tanaka has forgotten he's giving a lecture tomorrow at 8:30.
4. Do your brothers get along very well?
5. May 20, 1986,

Friday
1. a wide, happy smile
2. it seemed to take a long time for something to happen
3. leave me alone; don't bother me
4. from someone who should know; from the original source
5. fired him

Monday 26

Correct these sentences.

1. why cant he understand that we dont got no more to give him

_____

2. the sitter had to sing im a little teapot before suzie wood go to bed

_____

Use context clues to determine the meaning of the bolded word below.

3. My **meddlesome** neighbor is always telling me how to take care of my garden.

_____

Identify this part of a friendly letter.

4. Dear Aunt Mabel, _____

Find the prepositional phrase in the sentence.

5. Mr. Winslow takes messages for his boss.

☐ ☐ ☐

Tuesday 26

What is the proper abbreviation for fahrenheit?

1. far.   ft.   F.   F

Give a proper noun for each common noun.

2. city   _____

3. business   _____

Correct these sentences.

4. him and me was paid fifteen dollars for the work we done

_____

5. we dont got room for no more pets explained mother

_____

Wednesday 26

Correct these sentences.

1. why did you eat them chips dip and olives so close to lunch time

_____

2. have you drew a animal on the mural yet

_____

Give the comparative and superlative adjectives. (busy)

3. _____

What is the meaning of this figure of speech?

4. Don't worry about paying me back for the drink. The cost was just <u>chicken feed</u>.

_____

Give the complete subject of this sentence.

5. My artistic friend Ben creates exciting paintings using water colors.

Thursday 26

Write the pronouns that would replace the underlined nouns.

Have <u>Tomas and Susan</u> seen <u>the lizard</u>?
    1   **2**

1. _____

2. _____

Correct these sentences.

3. we aint got time now but well stop by this afternoon

_____

4. yes you can borrow my car but you must return it by 1100 pm

_____

Circle the cause and underline the effect.

5. Samantha missed the school bus, so Mother had to drive her to school.

Name:

Friday 26

Choose the best word to complete each sentence.

1. All week we camped out and _____ trout.
   catched   caught   was catching

2. Of all the desserts I've ever eaten, ice cream is the _____.
   good   better   best

3. Are you feeling _____ now?
   good   better   best

4. When will _____ plane arrive?
   their   there   they're

5. Did you know _____ both from Texas?
   their   there   they're

☐   ☐   ☐

Answer Key 26

Monday
1. Why can't he understand that we don't have any more to give him?
2. The sitter had to sing "I'm a Little Teapot" before Suzie would go to bed.
3. interferring
4. salutation (greeting)
5. for his boss

Tuesday
1. F
2. Answers will vary.
3. Answers will vary.
4. He and I were paid fifteen dollars for the work we did.
5. "We don't have room for any more pets," explained Mother.

Wednesday
1. Why did you eat those chips, dip, and olives so close to lunch time?
2. Have you drawn an animal on the mural yet?
3. busier, busiest
4. inexpensive; cheap; very little cost
5. My artistic friend Ben

Thursday
1. they
2. it
3. We haven't got time now, but we'll stop by this afternoon.
4. Yes, you may borrow my car, but you must return it by 11:00 p.m.
5. (Samantha missed the school bus,) so Mother had to drive her to school.

Friday
1. caught
2. best
3. better
4. their
5. they're

Monday 27

Correct these sentences.

1. a alligator caused a fright win it escaped from the bronx zoo

2. the reporter ask do ewe plan to run for re-election mr president

Subject pronoun or object pronoun?

3. Can you help <u>her</u> cross the street.

4. When will <u>they</u> be here?

What do these words have in common?

5. Monopoly   Parchesi   Sorry   Trivial Pursuit

Tuesday 27

Which part of speech is underlined in this sentence?

1. Everyone <u>scattered</u> when hail began to fall.

Give two words that rhyme with wonder.

2.

Correct these sentences.

3. the house shaked dishes rattled and the dog howled it was a earthquake

4. shes calling her friend jamie to see if he am ready to go

Synonyms, antonyms, or homophones?

5. frequent, often

Wednesday | 27

Correct these sentences.

1. rita found her favorite book island of the blue dolphins on a discount table

_____

2. her and i are spending tonight at camilles mountain cabin

_____

Add a prefix to this word.

3. cover _____

Where would the following probably take place?

4. "Open wide, please. I want to look at that molar." _____

Which two words need to be switched to make the list in correct alphabetical order?

5. laughter   laundry   legal   lovely   lightning

▢   ▢   ▢

Thursday | 27

Which words have the same sound as /i/ in mine?

1. rhyme   splinter   light   tie   cynic

Which word is a plural noun?

2. baby's   calves   ski

Correct these sentences.

3. the symphony begun at 700 and ended at 1030

_____

4. there dad has a new job so they has to move to atlanta georgia next month

_____

Give the past and future tenses for the verb speak.

5. _____

Which reference source would be best to look up the information: thesaurus, dictionary, telephone book, atlas, encyclopedia, or almanac?

1. information about the rings of Saturn

2. where the komodo dragon lives

3. an antonym for "glisten"

4. the street on which Paul and Kate Winslow live

5. the location of the Congo Basin

Daily Language Review

Answer Key **27**

Monday
1. An alligator caused a fright when it escaped from the Bronx Zoo.
2. The reporter asked, "Do you plan to run for re-election, Mr. President?"
3. object pronoun
4. subject pronoun
5. They are all board games.

Tuesday
1. verb
2. Answers will vary.
3. The house shook, dishes rattled, and the dog howled. It was an earthquake!
4. She's calling her friend Jamie to see if he is ready to go.
5. synonyms

Wednesday
1. Rita found her favorite book, Island of the Blue Dolphins, on a discount table.
2. She and I are spending tonight at Camille's mountain cabin.
3. recover, discover, uncover
4. at the dentist's office
5. lovely, lightning

Thursday
1. rhyme   light   tie
2. calves
3. The symphony began at 7:00 and ended at 10:30.
4. Their dad has a new job, so they have to move to Atlanta, Georgia, next month.
5. spoke, will speak

Friday
1. encyclopedia
2. encyclopedia
3. thesaurus
4. telephone book
5. atlas

Correct these sentences.

1. isaac broked the window but it was a accident he payed to have it fixed

2. the teams can begun to play as soon as the referees whistle is blowed

Use context clues to determine the meaning of the bolded word below.

3. They were arrested for **perpetrating** a crime at the 7-Eleven on the corner.

What is the root or base word?

4. plentiful

5. misfortune

What is the correct way to divide the word into syllables?

1. cel eb rate   cel e brate   ce le brate   ce leb rate

Correct these sentences.

2. while i was gone my puppy ate my cookies but she left my milk

3. do you wanna go to the movies or wood you rather go bowling

Is the subject or predicate underlined in this sentence?

4. Yesterday morning <u>Angela's pet hamster</u> escaped from its cage.

Does the underlined word have a prefix or a suffix?

5. Her parents were concerned about her <u>antisocial</u> behavior.

Wednesday 28

Correct these sentences.

1. the first long book i ever read was ramona the pest by beverly cleary

2. mr lundbergs class planted a oak tree along the walking trail on arbor day

Fact or opinion?

3. Bats are useful mammals.

Which word is NOT spelled correctly?

4. thought   suprise   principle   council

Which words are adverbs?

5. sooner   almost   hurry   tomorrow

☐   ☐   ☐

Thursday 28

Does the underlined adjective tell which one, what kind, or how many?

1. <u>That</u> old man ate small, red cherries one summer afternoon.

Fact or fantasy?

2. The Statue of Liberty was a gift to the United States from France.

Correct the sentences.

3. before going to work mrs bingham jogged around el estero park for times

4. on aug 14 dr agosto became head veterinarian at the san diego zoo

Simile or metaphor?

5. My brother is as <u>stubborn as a mule</u>.

Name:

Friday 28

Read the following paragraph and decide if the underlined parts have a capitalization error, a punctuation error, a spelling error, or no mistake.

When we <u>think of Antarctica we think</u> COLD! The mountains are icy; the plains are icy;
          1

the coastline <u>is icey. Most of the</u> continent is buried under thousands of meters
          2

<u>of ice and snow. High</u> winds blow the snow around. Ice sheets move <u>slowly from High Inland</u>
   3   **4**

areas down <u>to the see.</u>
       5

1. ....

2. ....

3. ....

4. ....

5. ....

☐ ☐ ☐

Answer Key 28

Monday
1. Isaac broke the window, but it was an accident. He paid to have it fixed.
2. The teams can begin to play as soon as the referee's whistle is blown.
3. committing
4. plenty
5. fortune

Tuesday
1. cel e brate
2. While I was gone, my puppy ate my cookies, but she left my milk.
3. Do you want to go to the movies, or would you rather go bowling?
4. subject
5. prefix

Wednesday
1. The first long book I ever read was <u>Ramona, the Pest</u> by Beverly Cleary.
2. Mr. Lundberg's class planted an oak tree along the walking trail on Arbor Day.
3. fact
4. suprise
5. sooner, almost, tomorrow

Thursday
1. which one
2. fact
3. Before going to work, Mrs. Bingham jogged around El Estero Park four times.
4. On Aug. 14, Dr. Agosto became head veterinarian at the San Diego Zoo.
5. simile

Friday
1. punctuation
2. spelling
3. no mistake
4. capitalization
5. spelling

 Daily Language Review Grade 5 EMC 583

Name: _____

Monday 29

Correct these sentences.

1. you may have a apple or a orange but you cant have both

_____

2. me and my sister gots to stay with ms papi while are parents are in germany

_____

Give the comparative and superlative forms of bad.

3. _____

Circle the words that rhyme.

4. seize   cease   squeeze   please   pause

Object pronoun or subject pronoun?

5. Uncle Louie wants <u>them</u> to help paint the fence.

☐   ☐   ☐

Name: _____

Tuesday 29

Circle the cause and underline the effect.

1. Amy broke her arm when she fell out of the treehouse.

Which words have the same sound as /a/ in plate?

2. strain   camera   freight   caught   prey

Correct these sentences.

3. latoyas birthday is on christmas day but she celebrates it on dec 26

_____

4. while most birds can flew kiwis penguins and ostriches cannot

_____

What reference source would you use to find the average snowfall in January in Nome, Alaska?

5. _____

Wednesday 29

Correct these sentences.

1. come hear zoe and help mrs aiello carry in them groceries

2. has you ever herd rev david taylor jr speak

What is this part of a business letter called?

3. Sincerely,
   William Smith

Find the prepositional phrase in the sentence.

4. Don't forget to put a stamp on the envelope.

Complete the analogy.

5. creche : Christmas :: menorah :

☐ ☐ ☐

Thursday 29

What is the correct abbreviation for manager?

1. a. man.   b. mr.   c. mgr.   d. none of these

Declarative, interrogative, imperative, or exclamatory?

2. Put that away before you leave

Correct these sentences.

3. a elephant was marching down main street wearing a sign advertising ringling brothers circus

4. the sidewalk was crowded as pedestrians was hurry to work to shop and to appointments

What is the correct way to divide the word into syllables?

5. am use ment   a mu se ment   a muse ment

Friday 29

Choose the best word to complete each sentence.

1. Pat and Mike _____ going fishing.
    was   were   is   wants

2. Mike was _____ the fishing poles.
    bring   brought   bringing

3. Pat _____ the first fish.
    catched   catching   caught

4. The fish was _____ small to keep.
    to   too   two

5. He _____ the tiny fish back into the water.
    through   threw   throwed

Answer Key 29

Monday
1. You may have an apple or an orange, but you can't have both.
2. My sister and I have to stay with Ms. Papi while our parents are in Germany.
3. worse, worst
4. seize, squeeze, please
5. object pronoun

Tuesday
1. <u>Amy broke her arm</u> when she fell ⟨out of the⟩ ⟨treehouse.⟩
2. strain   freight   prey
3. Latoya's birthday is on Christmas Day, but she celebrates it on Dec. 26.
4. While most birds can fly, kiwis, penguins, and ostriches cannot.
5. almanac

Wednesday
1. Come here, Zoe, and help Mrs. Aiello carry in those groceries.
2. Have you ever heard Rev. David Taylor, Jr. speak?
3. closing and signature
4. on the envelope
5. Hanukkah

Thursday
1. c. mgr.
2. imperative
3. An elephant was marching down Main Street wearing a sign advertising Ringling Brothers' Circus.
4. The sidewalk was crowded as pedestrians were hurrying to work, to shop, and to appointments.
5. a muse ment

Friday
1. were
2. bringing
3. caught
4. too
5. threw

Name:

Monday 30

Correct these sentences.

1. most of my friends like to play video games but rafik and me prefer chess

_____

2. rebecca can you come selling on our boat saturday were going at 600 am

_____

Use context clues to determine the meaning of the bolded word below.

3. The entire math class, including Prof. Smith, was **perplexed** by the difficult problem.

_____

Past, present, or future?

4. Phoebe <u>dreams</u> of being a ballerina someday. _____

What is the correct abbreviation for amount?

5. am.   at.   amn.   amt.

☐   ☐   ☐

Name:

Tuesday 30

Fact or opinion?

1. Rap is the greatest kind of music. _____

Give an antonym for anxious.

2. _____

Correct these sentences.

3. dr lee the pediatrician is always very gentle as she treats her young patience

_____

4. why is lee stella and corinne digging up them bushes in there back yard

_____

Use this homophone pair in one sentence. (scent, sent)

5. _____

Wednesday 30

Correct these sentences.

1. carlos lended his basketball to roberto and i we returned it after practice

_____

2. the teams uniforms was filthy after playing on that muddy field the players was dirty to

_____

Is the underlined word a noun, verb, adjective, or adverb?

3. The frightened puppy hid under the bed <u>during</u> the thunderstorm. _____

Which word IS spelled correctly?

4. eagar   fucher   boundary   ourselfs

Does the underlined adjective tell which one, what kind, or how many?

5. A <u>dozen</u> boys tried out for the team. _____

☐   ☐   ☐

Thursday 30

Past, present, or future?

1. The artist is having a showing of his work in the fall. _____

2. She flew to Brazil for Mardi Gras. _____

Correct these sentences.

3. mosquitos crickets and the howling of a wolf keeped the campers awoke most of the night

_____

4. why do i always have two give kiki a bath mother complained aaron

_____

Give the comparative and superlative adjectives. (lazy)

5. _____

Friday 30

Which reference source would be best to look up the information: thesaurus, dictionary, telephone book, atlas, encyclopedia, or almanac?

1. the origin of the word "dandelion"

2. the current population of Saudi Arabia

3. locations of pet shops in your home town

4. information about the Louisiana Purchase

5. the capital city of Quebec

Daily Language Review

Answer Key 30

Monday
1. Most of my friends like to play video games, but Rafik and I prefer chess.
2. Rebecca, can you come sailing on our boat Saturday? We're going at 6:00 a.m.
3. confused, bewildered, puzzled
4. present
5. amt.

Tuesday
1. opinion
2. calm, peaceful
3. Dr. Lee, the pediatrician, is always very gentle as she treats her young patients.
4. Why are Lee, Stella, and Corinne digging up those bushes in their back yard?
5. Answers will vary.

Wednesday
1. Carlos lent his basketball to Roberto and me. We returned it after practice.
2. The team's uniforms were filthy after playing on that muddy field. The players were dirty too.
3. adverb
4. boundary
5. how many

Thursday
1. future
2. past
3. Mosquitos, crickets, and the howling of a wolf kept the campers awake most of the night.
4. "Why do I always have to give Kiki a bath, Mother?" complained Aaron.
5. lazier, laziest

Friday
1. dictionary
2. almanac
3. telephone book
4. encyclopedia
5. atlas, encyclopedia

Monday 31

Correct these sentences.

1. because there was so many people we had two take to taxis

2. did they arrive in time to catch the plane inquired tomas yes they just made it ralph replied

Give synonyms for these words.

3. complete

4. sufficient

Does the underlined adverb tell when, how much, or where?

5. The doctor waited <u>patiently</u> for the test results.

Tuesday 31

What is the meaning of this figure of speech?
1. The third time the thief appeared in court, the judge <u>threw the book at him</u>.

Give two words that rhyme with caught.

2.

Correct these sentences.

3. im sorry he dont like the present i gave him

4. if this plan dont work well have to start all over agin

What do these words have in common?

5. bagel   croissant   pita   tortilla

Wednesday 31

Correct these sentences.

1. its naomis turn to lit the candles for hanukkah

2. hour town has a big parade on july 4 to celebrate independence day

Circle the cause and underline the effect.

3. I missed my flight connections because my plane was twenty minutes late getting into Chicago.

Write an opinion about this topic: snakes

4. _____

Which word is NOT spelled correctly?

5. arithmetic   traveling   wether   principal

▢   ▢   ▢

Thursday 31

What type of job is described here?

1. He replaced the leaking fuel pump and the worn brake pads on my car.

Use context clues to determine the meaning of the bolded word below.

2. That river has **meandered** through the canyons for thousands of years.

Correct these sentences.

3. her and otto has gone to male a package to grandma rosie

4. was you there when we sung yankee doodle in the school pageant

Underline the complete predicate of this sentence.

5. After a slow beginning, the farmer harvested the whole crop in one week.

Name:

Friday 31

Read the following paragraph and decide if the underlined parts have a capitalization error, a punctuation error, a spelling error, or no mistake.

Does it <u>surprise you, to learn</u> that <u>peanuts grow underground.</u> In some
      1   **2**

<u>countrys they are called</u> groundnuts. They are not really <u>nuts. they belong to</u> the same
    3   **4**

plant family as peas. What we eat are the <u>seeds of the peanut plant.</u>
                                                          5

1. _____

2. _____

3. _____

4. _____

5. _____

Answer Key 31

Monday
1. Because there were so many people, we had to take two taxis.
2. "Did they arrive in time to catch the plane?" inquired Tomas. "Yes, they just made it," Ralph replied.
3. finish
4. enough
5. how

Tuesday
1. The judge gave the thief the longest sentence allowed by law.
2. Answers will vary.
3. I'm sorry he didn't (or doesn't) like the present I gave him.
4. If this plan doesn't work, we'll have to start all over again.
5. They are all types of bread.

Wednesday
1. It's Naomi's turn to light the candles for Hanukkah.
2. Our town has a big parade on July 4 to celebrate Independence Day.
3. <u>I missed my flight connections</u> because my plane was twenty minutes late getting into Chicago.
4. Answers will vary.
5. wether

Thursday
1. automobile mechanic
2. wandered; followed a winding course
3. She and Otto have gone to mail a package to Grandma Rosie.
4. Were you there when we sang "Yankee Doodle" in the school pageant?
5. harvested the whole crop in one week

Friday
1. punctuation
2. punctuation
3. spelling
4. capitalization
5. no mistake

Monday 32

Correct these sentences.

1. mr watkins the custodian moved them students desks when he cleaned the room

_____

2. my niece is gonna get married on sept 13 1998

_____

Simile or metaphor?

3. That lazy boy was <u>as slow as molasses in January</u> when it came to doing his chores.

_____

Which word is NOT spelled correctly?

4. Angela's   I've   was'nt   children's

What time of day would this occur?

5. As the clock struck twelve, one lone car moved silently along the dark avenue.

_____

Tuesday 32

Give the possessive form.

1. suits of those astronauts

_____

Correct these sentences.

2. skagway yukon territory is a interesting town to visit

_____

3. our librarian mr talbot gave a book talk on the slave dancer

_____

Synonyms, antonyms, homophones?

4. arrival, departure _____

Put these words in correct alphabetical order.

5. disappoint   disaster   disagree   disarm   disable

Wednesday 32

Correct these sentences.

1. once the rain stopped phillip jack and me went to the park

2. ruth knitted a pear of slippers for mrs gee her neighbor

What two words make this contraction?

3. who'd

What part of speech is underlined in this sentence?

4. Wild rabbits <u>avoid</u> danger as often as possible.

Which word does not belong?

5. lobster   squid   anemone   shark   crab

Thursday 32

Use this homophone pair in one sentence. (sight, site)

1.

If the guide words on a page are "jaguar" and "jelly," which word would be found on the page?

2. jeopardy   jade   jealous   jersey   jackal

Correct these sentences.

3. mother red the wall street journal before she goed to work

4. during the earthquake they feeled the floor shook under there feet

Add a suffix to this word.

5. destruct

Combine the sentences to make one sentence.

1. Uncle Henry barbecued chicken.   He cooked it for dinner.   We ate all the chicken.

2. Eric wanted to play.   He wanted to play with his friends.   He had to mow the lawn first.

3. The chimpanzee was hungry.   It caught ants on a stick.   It ate the ants.

4. My cat kept throwing up.   I took him to see Dr. Arnold.   She is our vet.

5. Our team lost the game.   We were still proud.   We had played our best.

Daily Language Review

Answer Key 32

Monday
1. Mr. Watkins, the custodian, moved those students' desks when he cleaned the room.
2. My niece is going to get married on Sept. 13, 1998.
3. simile
4. was'nt
5. It is midnight.

Tuesday
1. astronauts' suits
2. Skagway, Yukon Territory, is an interesting town to visit.
3. Our librarian, Mr. Talbot, gave a book talk on <u>The Slave Dancer</u>.
4. antonyms
5. disable disagree disappoint disarm disaster

Wednesday
1. Once the rain stopped, Phillip, Jack, and I went to the park.
2. Ruth knitted a pair of slippers for Mrs. Gee, her neighbor.
3. who would
4. verb
5. shark – all the rest are invertebrates

Thursday
1. Answers will vary.
2. jealous
3. Mother read the <u>Wall Street Journal</u> before she went to work.
4. During the earthquake, they felt the floor shake under their feet.
5. destructive, destruction, destructible

Friday
Sentences may vary somewhat. Accept any reasonable sentence construction that contains all the information.
1. We ate all the chicken Uncle Henry barbecued for dinner.
2. Eric wanted to play with his friends, but he had to mow the lawn first.
3. The hungry chimpanzee caught ants on a stick and ate them.
4. My cat kept throwing up, so I took him to our vet, Dr. Arnold.
5. Our team lost the game, but we were still proud since we had played our best.

Correct these sentences.

1. i dont have nothing to put in the yard sail complained john

2. we seen dr chin in new orleans when we was on vacation

What is the base or root word?

3. uncomfortable

4. illogical

Underline the prepositional phrase in the sentence.

5. Did you get a letter from your pen pal?

Circle the complete predicate in this sentence.

1. The trained seal balanced a ball on its nose.

Use context clues to determine the meaning of the bolded word below.

2. Our pilot became concerned when he saw the dark, **ominous** sky.

Correct these sentences.

3. me and tom have three pets and they is all dogs

4. if anyone still needs a costume they can get won from the closet

Add a prefix to this word.

5. certain

Wednesday | 33 |

Correct these sentences.

1. uncle franks garden contained onions eggplants and zucchini last year

_____

2. we has drove to san francisco often our grandparents live their

_____

Complete the analogy.

3. humidity : hygrometer :: temperature : _____

Does the underlined adjective tell which one, how many, what kind?

4. How many of <u>those</u> people speak Japanese? _____

What reference source would you use to find the shortest route from Italy to Belgium?

5. _____

Thursday | 33 |

Give the pronoun that would replace the underline nouns in this sentence.

1. <u>Willie, Millie, and Tillie</u> are triplets. _____

Which word does not belong in this group?

2. sphere   cone   pyramid   triangle   cube

Correct these sentences.

3. stevens little sister lays down for a nap every day

_____

4. the novel oliver twist was wrote buy charles dickens

_____

Which part of speech is underlined?

5. The choir sang <u>joyfully</u> throughout the concert. _____

What do the underlined phrases mean?

1. When Mrs. Carter turned fifty years old she felt like <u>she was over the hill.</u>

2. My grandma always says, "<u>Time flies</u> when you're having fun."

3. Jeff and Maria don't <u>see eye to eye</u> on the best way to build the model.

4. "I'll do it <u>when the cows come home,</u>" said the lazy boy.

5. You've got <u>rocks in your head</u> if you think that will work!

Daily Language Review # Answer Key 33

Monday
1. "I don't have anything to put in the yard sale," complained John.
2. We saw Dr. Chin in New Orleans when we were on vacation.
3. comfort
4. logic
5. from your pen pal

Tuesday
1. balanced a ball on its nose
2. threatening, dangerous
3. Tom and I have three pets, and they are all dogs.
4. If anyone still needs a costume, he can get one from the closet.
5. uncertain

Wednesday
1. Uncle Frank's garden contained onions, eggplants, and zucchini last year.
2. We have driven to San Francisco often. Our grandparents live there.
3. thermometer
4. which one
5. atlas

Thursday
1. They
2. triangle, the rest are solid (three-dimensional) figures
3. Steven's little sister lies down for a nap every day.
4. The novel <u>Oliver Twist</u> was written by Charles Dickens.
5. adverb

Friday
1. She felt really old.
2. Time seems to move really fast when you're enjoying yourself.
3. They don't agree.
4. He'll do it much later. He'll put it off as long as possible.
5. You aren't thinking very well. You're not being very smart.

Correct these sentences.

1. by january our group will finished its report on sojourner truth

2. when father herd about the bad storms he cancelled hour skiing trip

Use context clues to determine the meaning of the bolded word below.

3. Father listens to the **meteorologist** forecast the day's weather as he drives to work.

What is the correct way to divide this word into syllables?

4. con clus ion   con clu sion   conclu sion   con clu si on

Where will the following probably take place?

5. Splendid Fellow galloped to victory, winning the race by a nose.

Give a fact about this topic: freckles

1.

If the guide words on a page were "human" and "humor," which word would NOT be on the page?

2. humerus   hummock   humorous   humidity   humble

Correct these sentences.

3. arnolds contribution was a large cold juicy watermelon

4. a old gnarled tree fell across bixby creek causing it to overflow

Does the underlined adverb tell how, when, where, or to what extent?

5. That woman <u>really</u> sang beautifully over there last night.

Wednesday 34

Correct these sentences.

1. when you presses that button a clown will pop up explained judy

2. neither him nor me were responsible for that mess he declared

Give the abbreviation for centimeter.

3.

Give the plural form for potato.

4.

Which word IS spelled correctly?

5. inflewence   influance   influence   enfluence

☐   ☐   ☐

Thursday 34

Give a common noun for this proper noun.

1. Saint Patrick's Day

Give the comparative and superlative forms of good.

2.

Correct these sentences.

3. im wearing millies read coat and shes wearing my blew sweater

4. that writers poem sea breezes was published in new yorker magazine

What is the following person's job?

5. Ms. Ramirez prepared blueprints of her ideas for a new office building.

Choose the best word to complete each sentence.

1. That was the _____ sandwich I have ever eaten.
   bad   baddest   worse   worst

2. Everyone _____ to catch the gold ring on the carousel.
   try   trying   tried   tryed

3. The gray horse ran _____ than the pinto.
   fast   faster   fastest   fastly

4. Kira is the _____ student in the fifth grade.
   young   younger   youngest   youthful

5. Is that the _____ test you've ever taken?
   difficult   difficulter   most difficult   difficulty

Monday
1. By January our group will have finished its report on Sojourner Truth.
2. When Father heard about the bad storms, he cancelled our skiing trip.
3. a scientist that studies weather and climate
4. con clu sion
5. a horse race

Tuesday
1. Answers will vary.
2. humorous
3. Arnold's contribution was a large, cold, juicy watermelon.
4. An old, gnarled tree fell across Bixby Creek causing it to overflow.
5. to what extent

Wednesday
1. "When you press that button, a clown will pop up," explained Judy.
2. "Neither he nor I was responsible for that mess!" he declared.
3. cm
4. potatoes
5. influence

Thursday
1. holiday
2. better, best
3. I'm wearing Millie's red coat, and she's wearing my blue sweater.
4. That writer's poem "Sea Breezes" was published in New Yorker Magazine.
5. architect

Friday
1. worst
2. tried
3. faster
4. youngest
5. most difficult

Monday [35]

Correct these sentences.

1. me and my brothers throwed a party for mother her birthday was friday aug 18

2. was he gave a ticket when he runned a red light

Complete the analogy.

3. wall : opaque :: window : _____

What contraction is made with these two words?

4. might have _____

Give the complete subject of this sentence.

5. A sudden storm took the campers by surprise last night.

☐ ☐ ☐

Tuesday [35]

Does this word have a suffix, a prefix, both, or none?

1. unsuccessful _____

Give another word that would be in this category.

2. Wilson   Hoover   Adams   Roosevelt   Reagan

Correct these sentences.

3. i aint never gonna sky dive again it was to scary

4. the chef chop a artichoke some butter lettuce and a red pepper into the salad bowl

What is the correct way to divide this word into syllables?

5. ast ron o my   as tro no my   as tron o my   as tro nom y

Wednesday 35

Correct these sentences.

1. how is a alligator and a crocodile different ask petes little sister

_____

2. school was cancelled when the temperature dropped to 40 f and the furnace breaked

_____

Give the present and future tenses of the verb meant.

3. _____   _____

Which word is NOT spelled correctly?

4. considerate   misrable   whistling   plotted

Synonyms, antonyms, or homophones?

5. absent, present   _____

□   □   □

Thursday 35

Give the comparative and superlative adjectives. (graceful)

1. _____   _____

Does the underlined adjective tell which one, what kind, or how many?

2. The <u>magnificent</u> mountains rose high into the azure sky.

_____

Correct these sentences.

3. sgt contreras and his family was thrilled when he one a million dollars in the lottery

_____

4. i dont want to touch them snakes tammy yelled her brother

_____

Fiction or nonfiction?

5. Finding a four-leaf clover will bring you good luck. _____

Friday 35

Which reference source would be best to look up the information: thesaurus, dictionary, telephone book, atlas, encyclopedia, or almanac?

1. to find the meaning of "azure"

2. on which continent Azerbaijan is located

3. another word for "peculiar"

4. information about the creation of national parks in the U.S.A.

5. all of the area codes for the county in which you live

Answer Key 35

Monday
1. My brothers and I threw a party for Mother. Her birthday was Friday, Aug. 18.
2. Was he given a ticket when he ran a red light?
3. transparent
4. might've
5. a sudden storm

Tuesday
1. both
2. Answers will vary but must name a president.
3. I am (or I'm) never going to sky dive again. It was too scary!
4. The chef chopped an artichoke, some butter lettuce, and a red pepper into the salad bowl.
5. as tron o my

Wednesday
1. "How are an alligator and a crocodile different?" asked Pete's little sister.
2. School was cancelled when the temperature dropped to 40°F and the furnace broke.
3. mean, will mean
4. misrable (miserable)
5. antonyms

Thursday
1. more graceful, most graceful
2. what kind
3. Sgt. Contreras and his family were thrilled when he won a million dollars in the lottery.
4. "I dont want to touch those snakes, Tammy!" yelled her brother.
5. fiction

Friday
1. dictionary
2. atlas
3. thesaurus
4. encyclopedia
5. telephone book

Name:

Monday 36

Correct these sentences.

1. mama likes to sang billy boy to me and my brother bill

2. because we was born on the same day tanisha and i is having our party together

Common noun or proper noun?

3. Kelly taught her nieces how to play <u>Chutes and Ladders</u>.

Metaphor or simile?

4. Dad was angry when his new car turned out to be <u>a lemon</u>.

Which word has the most syllables?

5. arrangement   thanksgiving   photography   orchestra

Name:

Tuesday 36

Which word IS spelled correctly?

1. envirement   environment   invironment   envirunment

Correct these sentences.

2. pete the lifeguard jump into the pool too rescue the ladys poodle

3. when george send me his new address ill right him a letter

What is the correct abbreviation for sergeant?

4. sar.   sarg.   srt.   sgt.

Where would this statement probably be heard?

5. "Would you like me to check your tires and look under the hood?"

Wednesday 36

Correct these sentences.

1. shall i take ballet lessons or study the french horn this year wondered megan

2. after seeing jurassic park jason ask do you think scientist will really clone dna to make a living dinosaur

Give an opinion about this topic: violence on television

3.

Identify the type of sentence.

4. The president gave a speech in Washington this morning.

Synonyms, antonyms, or homophones?

5. while, during

Thursday 36

If the guide words on a page are "relative" and "relief," which words would NOT be found on the page?

1. release   reliable   rejoice   relieve   relax

Add a suffix to this word.

2. hope

Correct these sentences.

3. is it a arduous climb to the top of mt mckinley eli wanted to no

4. after watching a vampire movie eli woke up screaming no no dont suck my blood

Fact or opinion?

5. Everybody should drink at least three glasses of milk a day.

Read the following paragraph and decide if the underlined parts have a capitalization error, a punctuation error, a spelling error, or no mistake.

President Teddy Roosevelt was quite <u>a hunter but</u> once refused to <u>shoot a bare cub</u>.

1   **2**

News of this <u>inspired a Cartoon which</u>, in turn, inspired <u>a toy manufacturer</u> to create — you

3   **4**

guessed it — <u>the Teddy Bear.</u>

            5

1. _____

2. _____

3. _____

4. _____

5. _____

Monday
1. Mama likes to sing "Billy Boy" to my brother Bill and me.
2. Because we were born on the same day, Tanisha and I are having our party together.
3. proper noun
4. metaphor
5. photography

Tuesday
1. environment
2. Pete, the lifeguard, jumped into the pool to rescue the lady's poodle.
3. When George sends me his new address, I'll write him a letter.
4. sgt.
5. at a gas/filling station

Wednesday
1. "Shall I take ballet lessons or study the French horn this year?" wondered Megan.
2. After seeing <u>Jurassic Park</u>, Jason asked, "Do you think scientists will really clone DNA to make a living dinosaur?"
3. Answers will vary but must express an opinion.
4. declarative
5. synonyms

Thursday
1. rejoice and relieve
2. hopeless, hopeful, hoping, hoped
3. "Is it an arduous climb to the top of Mt. McKinley?" Eli wanted to know.
4. After watching a vampire movie, Eli woke up screaming, "No! No! Don't suck my blood!"
5. opinion

Friday
1. no mistake
2. spelling
3. capitalization
4. no mistake
5. no mistake